IMPERFECT
FAMILY

Setting Free Skeletons of Kinship Neglect

LEYLAND A. KING

Gotham Books

30 N Gould St.
Ste. 20820, Sheridan, WY 82801
https://gothambooksinc.com/

Phone: 1 (307) 464-7800

© 2024 *Leyland A. King*. All rights reserved.

No part of this book may be reproduced, stored in a retrieval system, or transmitted by any means without the written permission of the author.

Published by Gotham Books (July 18, 2024)

ISBN: 979-8-88775-560-1 (P)
ISBN: 979-8-88775-561-8 (E)

Because of the dynamic nature of the Internet, any web addresses or links contained in this book may have changed since publication and may no longer be valid.

The views expressed in this work are solely those of the author and do not necessarily reflect the views of the publisher, and the publisher hereby disclaims any responsibility for them.

TABLE OF CONTENTS

CHAPTER I SAYING GOOD-BYE 1
CHAPTER II TIME FOR MY DUTY 11
CHAPTER III THE SON ALBERT 14
CHAPTER IV THE KING'S HOUSEHOLD 18
CHAPTER V BROKEN CHILDREN, BROKEN PARENTS, BROKEN CHILDREN 35
CHAPTER VI SPARE THE ROD, LOVE THE CHILD 51
CHAPTER VII CARRYING THE BATON, COMPLETING THE RELAY 60
CHAPTER VIII LIFE'S ROTATING WHEEL 66
CHAPTER IX OUR VISIT TO HIS FATHER 78
CHAPTER X A VISIT TO ROSE HALL ESTATE 99
CHAPTER XI MAKING LEMONADE 106
CHAPTER XII DUTY BOUND 116
CHAPTER XIII SHARING THE PAIN 122
CHAPTER XIV IT'S ALL CONNECTED 135
CHAPTER XV A FINER SIDE 153
CHAPTER XVI LISTEN AND LEARN 157
CHAPTER XVII HE PLAYED WITH FIRE TOO 168
CHAPTER XVIII WOULD SOMEONE PLEASE RAISE THE ADULTS 177
CHAPTER XIX SECURING ONE'S OWN BONDAGE 190
CHAPTER XX THE DAY IT RAINED & DROWN THE PROFLIGATE 194
CHAPTER XXI FILIAL DUTY HONORED AT ALL COST 200
CHAPTER XXII BEHIND EVERY SUCCESSFUL WOMAN 212
CHAPTER XXIII WHAT DID WE BELIEVE 225

CHAPTER XXIV IT MAY BE MUCH DARKER THAN IT SEEMS 232
CHAPTER XXV REVELING IN ANOTHER'S TROUBLE 240
CHAPTER XXVI INTERLOCK EFFECTUATED........................ 251
EPILOGUE 260

DEDICATION

To my beloved parents, *Albert Edward King* and *Elaine Aletha King,* who toiled indefatigably and who, by their industry, elevated themselves from privation, despite the suffocating pressures of tribulation. Their ambition and their sacrifices were all aimed at providing for my siblings and me a better life than was handed them. We have so much to thank them for.

ACKNOWLEDGMENTS

My LOVE & APPRECIATION to my siblings, Carmen, Dennis, Cecil, Doreen, and Mayleen. Sharing ties with you in our humble home was fun. I hope you don't mind a visit to what's past. It would please me immeasurably should my children—Fiona King, Marvin King, Aretha Richardson, Gavin King, and Mariel King—find something explanatory, encouraging, and humorous herein. In fact, I would be glad should they encounter anything that clarifies what might be known but never discussed. Hopefully, my seven grandchildren, having grown tired of social media, will one day give this book some attention.

Thanks to my wife, Kathy King, for empathic listening, for her patient support, and for being tremendously understanding and giving me space as necessary to finish what I'd committed to do. Thank you to Miss Kennedi Barbery for her interest in my writing.

My gratitude to my kind, loving, longtime friends Erica Johnson and Chevelle (Washington) Howard for their suggestions and patient persuasions when my spirit sank, and my completion of this book seemed doubtful.

PREFACE

MULLING OVER THE idea to create a written account of our family remained just that for quite some time—mulling. I do not know when the decision to write this book was actually made. It might have been a germ of an idea that developed gradually after my father died, or it may have been inspired by the flash experience of having looked in the mirror one ordinary day and met my father's appraising eyes—figuratively, of course. Others have commented on how much my son, Marvin, has my features, and I, my father's. That might have been the spark needed to do it now or regret it later.

Whatever the prompt, I am so grateful and happy I had the privilege of returning to times and places long past, this time more informed than I was when the events I revisited first occurred, and of picking up pieces here and there and collating them as best I know how. Ultimately, I am grateful to offer, for my reader and for our families, a coherent biographical record of my family's household and relationships and many significant events of the King family. The self-understanding I derived from the exercise is invaluable.

In so doing, I faced several challenges, some I willingly embraced, others enigmatic and troubling, and some vexing. At one point, I developed a three-week aversion to my computer and could not write one word; I was emotionally rattled. But then I experienced two cathartic episodes, which made it all the more worthwhile to have completed this memorial.

During one, I gained a better understanding of the lasting power of intergenerational loyalty, neglect, struggles, and conflict. The second was when, for the first time since my father's death years earlier, I had a terror-free dream of him. I was glad for that because so much had been left unresolved between us. Yes, we had lots of unfinished business. I hope the reader will find this account as interesting as I do.

One surprising aspect of writing Imperfect Family was my firsthand encounter with the degree to which memory is edited and reconstructed. It was fascinating to truly know how fallible our memories are. I was able to appreciate that, among our family of eight, there are eight different accounts of what our home was like. Only after I'd shifted to observe events from multiple perspectives, particularly using interviewees' eyes, did the biography became a story able to be sincerely told. Eight pairs of eyes and eight differing accounts gave me parts of crucial experiences, remembered in edited versions, unreliable interpretations, and imprecise meaning. It was like careless winds had come and sucked up or warped one's recollections, but I made up for the loss by cross-checking anything appearing to be substantive. My sister Mayleen was an invaluable resource of information, most helpful in stitching together episodes I should have but did not remember and thereby enabling the best biographic quilt possible.

As we recalled various elements of events and built the story and drawing on my experiences as a commissioned police officer and those I'd had during my second career as a child protective investigations program administrator, I came to presume that there is no perfect family. However, there are multitudes of families who have become very skilled at concealing the unflattering details, while parading commendable portions of their lives. Imperfect beings cannot have perfect unions. Thus, the notion that "they lived happily ever after" ought to be interred in Fableland.

The reader will learn of traumatic events, callousness, and child rearing indifference, of kinship duties unfulfilled and respect dishonored. In this book, one may also learn positive behaviors worth emulating, such as parsimony, hospitality, adherence to filial responsibilities, reciprocity, and self-mastery.

I tried to balance this book with some folklore and levity, but that ought not be construed as mocking or making light of the very serious autobiographical history of our family. In fact, these tales complement the work, if only because we are all integrated into and affected by our cultural ethos.

CHAPTER I

SAYING GOOD-BYE

For children preserve the fame of a man after his death.
— Aeschylus

IT MUST HAVE been a shock to my father when I informed him that I was leaving our home. At age fifty-six, divorce imminent, he must have found that his family, for whom he had provided, was suddenly disintegrating. His job was signaling it would soon be time to retire. His house, built from his pocket, had pressing needs. My father seemed powerless to deal with all the changes. The truth is, he would have no one but himself to blame for the series of events that would transpire.

It took me a long time to realize that my father was not ready to see me leave home, despite our explosive relationship, especially at that time, and even more so after Mommy left. It would be inaccurate to describe emotions then as anything like a roller coaster, since that ride's peaks, plunges, twists, and turns are predictable and familiar. One chooses the thrill of the event. The screams are those of joyous excitement, and then it's over too soon. So, I'd rather describe the emotions we experienced at that time as a train wreck—in slow motion. Slowly, thundering, heaving as it comes, a train and its arrival will be, for some, a disastrous collision.

For my father and me, our interaction, in fact our relationship, was in other ways dissimilar to the ride. Neither of us consented to embark; nor could we get off. And while the valleys held real-life consequences, the peaks could not be trusted. Our relationship might best be illustrated as unnervingly erratic. Yes, that was it. If that were not bad enough, the environment was often punctuated by periods of flat desolation, much like an empty, silent, arid place, stifling any affectionate initiatives.

I spent years trying to resolve the issue without gaining as much as a good guess. Then, as I began gathering odds and ends to commence writing this memoir, I was compelled to shift my perspective and began to see our world primarily through my father's eyes. It was not pretty. The enigma suddenly unraveled and struck me with the clarity of an epiphany. My father loved and needed me more at that time than I could ever have imagined. Neither could he, I guess. So incredulously stubborn were we both and talk of feelings so discouraged that we did not know. We could not have known. To construct this biography, much had to be deduced from the assembled bits and pieces of his life's portrait.

The first good-bye I said to him seemed to be met with the cold shoulder of indifference. It happened the night after my sister Dolly's wedding. It was a cool November Sunday. The reception, held at my sister's godmother's residence (we called her Sister Stella), had been managed without the incident we feared. Our fears centered on the fact that our parents had already separated, and both were expected to attend. We knew Daddy was upset about that and had been brooding about it.

He was alone at home in the shower room when I arrived. He appeared to be going through his rituals for bed, evident by his pajamas. He moved with slow deliberation. Daddy's demeanor indicated a solemn mood; he was overly distant and did not appear interested in seeing me or talking. My father had completely withdrawn into himself.

Sitting on the kitchen stairs and with him a few feet away, I announced that I was joining the police force and would be leaving for Georgetown later that night to report to the police training school.

"Daddy, I received a telephone message from the police force, telling me I was accepted. I have to report there on Monday morning."

He was briefly quiet. "The police force," he muttered flatly, as if just thinking out loud. He stood in the middle of the kitchen, looking down at the worn linoleum as if contemplating the years-old designs for the first time.

"Yes," I replied, hoping he'd be glad, proud maybe, and would say something praiseworthy or encouraging. He chose instead to douse the occasion with a bucket of ice water and a small measure of criticism.

"Couldn't you find something to do around here?" I sensed he was showing interest only because it was the proper thing to do. Strange question, I thought, since he'd frowned on the two bartending jobs I'd had since leaving the post office. But I didn't argue or show emotion. We had passed the worst of that disagreement some time before. He had also been displeased with my going overnight to the bauxite mines, where a friend had been secretly teaching me to operate a front-end excavation machine in the hope that I would develop skills relevant to the company. The machine was a huge, intimidating, Caterpillar earthmover with enormous wheels, the diagonal of which tested my height. A little ladder attached to the right side aided my climb to the driver's seat.

As a recent event had shown us, Daddy was absolutely right in his judgment about the risks of going to the mines. But I needed work. Please bear with the digression. One night, while roaring to the dig site at the beginning of the shift, I was propelled headlong toward a point beneath the machine's massive rear wheels. The vehicle bounced and lurched, a breath away from being out of control on the dark, unfinished road. This happened as a combination of my precarious perch on the panel beside the driver's seat and my friend Boodie's recklessness. I concluded that he wanted to show off since there had been no reason to rush. However, he probably saved my life as he had the strength, dexterity, and mental acuity to swiftly extend his left arm, grab the back of my collar, and yank me back into the cab. All this he did in seconds while steering, slowing, and stabilizing the heavy- duty machine. That was the last of about four times I went to the mines. We had an unspoken agreement that a second scare was really unnecessary since we had learned our lessons.

My attention returned to my father. "No," I said to him, adding politely, "I've been to the employment office many times. I was always turned down, no matter how early I got there." I would arrive at 6:00 a.m. for interviews beginning at 9:00 a.m.

He paused again. He walked past me, each step up the kitchen stairs purposeful; laborious might be more accurate. Daddy then said resignedly, "Well, if that's what you want to do." After a moment's silence, he added under his breath, "I have nothing to give you." He went slowly to bed, alone in the house. I wondered if he cried in bed; he had appeared so dispirited. Such describes my first good-bye.

His last son was leaving home. Five of his six children were now gone.

I was not surprised, though a bit stung, by his dismissiveness— not mad, just a little disappointed in him not being proud of me for earning acceptance into the police force or even giving me a dollar for my journey. After all, it had been a long process of interviews, measurements, and medical examinations by day and one at night. Then there had been the hopeful lineup for actual selection by the commissioner of police and his team. I'd paid for all the travel and accommodations. About a third of the candidates had been successful. I was passed over at first. I knew it was because I was too skinny, but the commissioner's aide, following with a thick clipboard, quickly mentioned to him that I had a general certificate of education (accredited by University of London) and a few certificates from the London Chamber of Commerce. The commissioner, a brawny man of six feet plus, stopped. He walked back and stood before me with a reappraising eye. Second look done, he growled, "Okay, you're in, but you have to put on some pounds." Then he moved along the line. Elation!

I was proud of my accomplishment and a bit scared too. I suppose my expectations of my father had been so lowered by then that his damp indifference should not have been unanticipated. Such was the emotional distance we had reached.

I departed our home a few minutes later without receiving so much as a handshake, a congratulatory word, or a wish for a safe journey. My luggage consisted of a small, black, and gray satchel. I had in my pocket $1.10, which I had reserved for the trip, and hope. I had an abundance of hope. That's right, the sum of my capital at the time was $1.10 and hope abundant. The fare I paid was $1.04, a second-class ticket on the night steamer.

I arrived in our capital city, Georgetown, with six cents in my pocket. I survived the month on meals from the mess hall and credit from the police canteen. From there I bought toothpaste, shoe polish, hair pomade, and a protein supplement. My determination to measure up to the 175 other trainees, divided into squads, served me well. I survived, succeeded, and was not mad at my father.

Without a doubt, his actions seemed callous to me then. As I gave it more thought, I modified that upward to inconsiderate. You may lift that further to, say, thoughtless when you begin to understand what may have been his motivation, or lack thereof.

Our father had been confronting more than his fair share at the time I went to say good-bye. He had given his all, and I was, in fact, the fifth of his six children to be leaving home. Two had migrated out of the country and one had in-migrated to the city. Dolly, my sister, had left the previous day for her new home and family. Our father's wife of over thirty years had just left him. Until one empathizes with his situation—that is, fully appreciates the rapid, harrowing, shaming disintegration of his family—his actions would not be mitigated. In fact, he was darned courageous given all that was happening. I suppose he imagined himself abandoned, all but Pinkey now gone. His senior years were fast approaching, and from where he stood then, he would have been seeing, stretching out before him, an unfathomable lonesomeness in an empty house.

My father's personality appeared to be classically authoritarian, melancholic, and passive-aggressive, which I would later come to learn. I did not arrive at this conclusion by any means of professional mental health diagnosis; it is merely speculative, based on the work I did. It might have appeared to him that, despite all his caring and self-sacrifice for his family, he was being compensated with small, cold, leaden coins of ungratefulness. All such life reviews and evaluative projections invariably have a tiny kernel of bitter truth. He had worked hard his entire life; he'd stuck by his family dutifully, despite problems not always of his making, and he had more often been the one sacrificing.

He bought little personal effects, choosing a simple life for himself. Daddy had one suit, a black one that he wore to funerals. The rest of his wardrobe consisted of a tie and a couple of white shirts, of course; sparing casuals; and his work clothes, mainly khaki or other durable material. To work, he wore metal-tipped safety boots and a hat or a cap, the latter replaced only after it was too worn for its purpose. A pair of black, well-built leather shoes completed his ensemble for those special occasions. He used to have me polish them when needed, which was very infrequent. Though ostentatious wristwatches were very fashionable at the time, enough to keep a repair shop on Arvida Road in steady business, my father never owned a watch. He never wore a ring, a chain, or a gold bracelet. In fact, he shunned adornments.

As far as it was possible to detect, he never kept a woman and went out very rarely without my mother. Family friends were almost all my mother's. I know of none he cultivated independently. But he did have workmates, of course.

Such a man would recall his own duty and generosity and then twist them to fit his own definition of his victimization and desertion. For all he gave, he now hardly received a letter from his children, save a missive from Carmen. My good-bye must have been received as desertion, one more stone weighing and wearing the martyr's gunnysack, proving his long settled, fortified, and reinforced opinion, born of a flawed argument's conclusion: *all are leaving me; therefore, nobody cares about me.*

CHAPTER II

TIME FOR MY DUTY

THERE IS AMPLE time for thinking while on an international flight. This was no pleasure trip, though. I was on my way from Florida to Guyana to visit my ailing father. According to my sister Pinkey, he had been admitted to hospital with concern that he might not survive. I wanted to be there before he passed. Traveling first-class was expensive, more so at short notice. Well, so be it. Gouge me with your fare; I have a duty to meet, and the occasion does not repeat.

In the quiet, unaccustomed luxury, the mind gets restless, and it roams; memories evince a smile here, a frown there, and moist eyes once or twice. Then suddenly, with lucidity, an unwanted scene just leaps in from nowhere, bullying your attention and mood. It's time again to do what all humans do—revisit the past.

I am not very attached to things—not the kind of person you'll ever encounter collecting in an antique store or buying celebrities' memorabilia. In fact, I think that a foolish, self-indulgent, glorification—a waste of time and money. Reminiscences, nostalgia need no objects. I ruminate just fine, thank you.

I reflected on when I had begun preparing for my trip. I had been clearing a cluttered drawer when I'd set aside my own certificate of birth, which had become less precious as years went by. I recalled that the document had been requisite for almost every little business needing to be done. Now it was old, thumb-worn, unneeded; it had yellowed in various shades, blotches of brown dotted it here and there, and it was falling apart at the four crosswise folds but held in place by pieces of adhesive tape. Its best days had gone, its purpose fulfilled. But the jet-black ink stayed bold, and the careful chirography, like the embossed seal, remained an admirably affirming symbol of authority. I looked at the thick sheet of bond paper wherefore a once proud civil servant had legitimized me in place, time, and class in the world and particularly British Guiana, a colony of the empire.

The record authenticated my arrival to married parents—that each of us was a "Black, Native of British Guiana," and that my father, Albert Edward King's occupation was "Laborer." There was no section requiring

Mother's line of work. The omission assumed women's role of that time; and certainly, we were not citizens of anywhere, literally. Albert's wife, my mother, was Elaine Aletha King nee Payne. Payne was her father's name. He had gone his own way and never once looked back. In fact, he'd never even made the time to see his baby girl.

Looking to an infinite sky, so blue on this bright day, and filled with big, cottony cumulus clouds, I thought of my father and appreciated how different our worlds were. I was grateful to him. And I thought how, but for his steadfastness; his sacrifices; and his character, shaped by his beliefs, I would not have had the privileges I enjoy—and how, but for his children, he and our mother would not have enjoyed the dignified later lives they were afforded.

CHAPTER III

THE SON ALBERT

IF THERE IS a metaphysical realm where waiting cherubs flit, seeking portals to wombs with promise of reasonably good lives, Albert Edward somehow must have been reckless in his choosing. He elected to alight in the capitol, Georgetown, and sometime later moved to the County of Berbice, Village of East Canje, to be precise, a sparsely populated settlement with no streetlights, poorly lit homes, and no plumbing of any kind. One collected rain in barrels or fetched water, a bucket a trip, from creeks or canals—those were abundant. Sometimes one would find a rare community spigot beside the road. The more fortunate residents, like his father, had huge wooden vats for storing water channeled from their roof's runoff. If ever there were a place where life's opportunities were minimal, even dismal, this was it.

Canje was an agricultural area dependent on Plantation Rose Hall, owned by Booker Company of London. Life was dominated by the sugar factory. Whether the factory was "grinding," "slow," or "on target" had, to the villagers, the level of importance comparable to a website and the electricity down at your corporation on the day prior to payday. The area was, in fact, one expansive plantation with a determinant culture that held one's life aspirations in a vise. Even if you grew cash crops or had a cake shop, a liquor business, or a grocery store, you were, in one way or another, inextricably tied to the plantation. At that time, sugar production was stupendously labor intensive, and profits marginal. That led to maximizing labor productivity and minimizing wages.

When the seasonal rains came, May to June and December to February, the unpaved roads turned to thick, red, or gray mud, depending on which you traversed, with lots of puddles to pick and lightly skip one's way through. Downpours and flooding challenged even the hardy.

At Canje Village, you rose before the sun to welcome the biting sand flies. Everything wanted to eat you or drink your blood. At sundown, the dark swarms of mosquitoes arrived with their ominous, familiar buzz for their share of the feast, leaving behind filaria, malaria, and yellow fever just to malevolently remind you of their visits. They pestered the horses, mules, donkeys, sheep, and any living thing they perceived as a banquet. Twitch, slap, and swat all you wanted; the thousands just kept coming. The residents burned coconut husks and dried dung to smoke them away. That gave some relief, shooing them hence. In the evening, people carried mosquito brooms with the stereotypical ubiquitous fashion of an Englishman and his umbrella. If you could imagine a horse's oversize tail consisting of straw and a plaited top binding them all together, you have the right representation of what the brooms looked like. They were effective though. The luckless insects died either by the blow or through hopeless entanglement in the hundreds of light straw strands of the broom.

Little Albert Edward got the place wrong and did no better with the scheduling. The few years before his birth were chaotic worldwide. British Guiana was not exempt from the prodigious power transitions that were occurring. Though in a distant continent, Britain and whatever affected her had enormous resonance in the colony. Let's take a quick look at the world of Albert's birth. It was a mere seventy-four years since the Slavery Abolition Amendment Act of 1838. Stating the obvious, one now had to pay people for services rendered and at competitive wages— or conjure apprenticeship rules, indentured servitude, trickery, or peonage to continue doing business. Some ex-slaves struck out on their own, farming or going into the country's interior in search of gold, diamonds, and other valuable stones. Some went to bleed milky, white balata for rubber factories overseas. Others pooled money and purchased land, consequentially exacerbating the deficit of labor resource availability. Industrialization also impacted labor, and capitalism ran amok.

CHAPTER IV

THE KING'S HOUSEHOLD

I THOUGHT OF my family of origin, my father in particular. Seven children were born to my parents. Kenrick immediately preceded me. He died of pneumonia when he was about four months old. His siblings then were Carmen, the eldest, and then Dennis and Cecil. My two sisters, Doreen, and Mayleen, were grouped with me, perhaps because of our closer ages. Sometimes I think that Kenrick's demise split the bonding in the family so that it was like two families under the same corrugated sheet metal roof. I had to deal with that and compete with deceased Kendrick in spite of my not even being born during the short time he lived. Typical of parents who lose a child of tender years, my parents viewed the departed's angelic ascension and handsomeness as exceeding the prior unsurpassable qualities they'd described at the previous telling of his attributes. Everything said of him was impossibly flattering and hyperbolic. It did not help that one of my sisters sometimes expressed her wish to trade me in for him.

Ah, kids.

One sociologist, the late Robert Merton, recognized the contribution of birth order to family dynamics. Ours appear to have exemplified the best and worse of that.

All of us children had to address our eldest sibling as Sister Carmen, the appellation conferring a status of respect. This was important because she was the parent in our own parents' absence. She had most of the dinner chores and was emotionally close to both of our parents. Dennis and Cecil had no prefixes or fond names. They were part of the first subfamily.

Each of us in the second subset had fond names. I was "Brods," sometimes "Brother."

Doreen was called "Doll" or "Dolly" and is to this day. We believed it was because she was so cheeked and very light skinned. As a baby, her hair was wispy and of light color. Everyone adored Dolly, the apple of Daddy's eye, who could do no wrong. Dolly was pretty, robust, and pugnacious. When we were young children, her unprovoked physical attacks on me were regarded mirthfully by my parents and, therefore, by all others in the home. I knew I could not hit back hard because, should I, admonition was swift— on me. Unbelievable! Even though everyone in the home was witnessing her aggression, mind you—she would hit me over the head with a shoe or anything at hand, for example—I had no choice but to submit. I had to lose the fight, which was worsened when the others would then taunt me for being beaten by a girl. In that situation of familial scapegoating, the lower child (me, in this case) has to act as if such untenable circumstance is all part of humorous play. The alternative was to learn to anticipate a clash and evade the looming threat. I employed this strategy, when necessary, if possible. It was sound preparation for sissy-hood or overcompensation of maleness. So, quiet rascal that I was, I chose to become a determined male. Her attacks would later come to, for her, a painful end.

Mayleen was called "Pinkey". She had a special relationship with our mother. We supposed it was because she had been born at seven months and had to have intensive medical care, and my mother must have been so afraid to lose her like Kenrick. Dolly and I knew very early on not to tell Pinkey a secret and certainly not to upset her in the slightest. If we each had a penny and bought snacks, she wanted her money back after she ate the treat. Pinkey, young as she was, knew the rules and advantages. She could cry on cue. All she had to do was make that special "pre-cry" sound with her tongue between her teeth, and we had to quickly mollify her, or our mother would arrive like an irate hen with an antennae having a bad day.

As we grew older, when Dolly and I had a squabble, she was smart enough to enjoin her powerful ally, Pinkey. She would turn to Pinkey and merely urge, "Girl, Pinkey girl, cry." Immediately, as called upon, the little one would deliver that fearsome "heeeshhhing" sound. It would start low, gradually amplified as they gauged my compliance with what they wanted. The looming threat would fast become real for me as Pinkey got the right pitch, and I would have to hastily put some distance between us. Skilled French diplomats can only aspire to the intellectual nimbleness, creative leveraging, and coercion that these two little devils had. But we three hung together, and I loved them both.

Daddy used to call Pinkey "Pinks." When he was in a really buoyant mood, he called her "Miss Voracious." The story behind that nickname has it that she had to be fed quite a lot to survive as a preemie. I wondered how hard that must have been for my parents, in fact for all of us. After all, the new baby was drinking up all the milk and, not sated with that, garnered all the attention. Just to be crystal clear, two well-favored princesses followed me in birth order, and before me was the flawless, sainted

Kenrick. Well, such a pickle is not good for one's ego development. Soon I realized parental expectations of me could never be met. Thinking about what was, led me to ponder on what ought to have been. I combed religious and secular literature with reference to parent- child relationships. I found that traditional guidance was best enunciated in the Holy Bible's Book of Ephesians:

"Children obey your parents in the Lord, for this is right. Honor your father and mother that it may go well with you and that you may live long in the land. Fathers, do not provoke your children to anger; instead, bring them up in the discipline and instruction of the Lord."

— Ephesians: 6:1-4

Discipline in our split-family household was abnormally capricious, harsh, and biased—maybe in part due to my parents having preferred children, a disposition that may or may not have been intentional. It seemed that Carmen was never physically disciplined by either parent. At least, I never saw it. She was special to both parents. Carmen and I never really played together, and we other kids had to obey her. My mother would never hit Dennis. Cecil and I were fair game. We had no white knights. We did not seem to merit "a good talking to."

With Daddy, that would not suffice, since he always reminded us that he would make us "as straight as an arrow." The floggings that Dennis and Cecil endured from my father I would wish on no creature. My father's primary instrument was a thick, heavy, broad, rough, leather belt; sometimes a cane would serve the purpose. The typical episode lasted about half an hour, each stroke on their bare buttocks. Daddy would put a chair in about the middle of the living room and each of my brothers got his turn bending across the chair, pantless. My father's hand raised high, the instrument would whistle down, ending abruptly with a sickening smack on the bare flesh. They would scream and beg. The rest of us would watch in sympathetic silence. Then Daddy would pace back and forth lecturing. One knew the next lash was about to come by the increased tone of his voice and quickened speech. Sometimes they would run out of the house, and Daddy would chase them on the street, whipping as they ran. It was better to go first and be spared the spectacle. My sisters would cry empathically; my mother would look out the window; I would be frozen with terror. When done, Daddy would look at me threateningly saying, "And you, mister, had better be careful." I would quake. Even though I had done nothing wrong, my father was threatening me. Incredible! That was all it took to keep me in line and fearful.

My mother would speak to him afterward. She did not condone his beatings, but she knew she must not interrupt, thus risking worse. I don't think the situation changed much, but boys develop quickly in their teens. I guess that stopped the flogging—that along with the fact that we hindered my father's choices of punishment by hiding the offending instruments, one at a time, in the guttering on the roof.

I know that Daddy's behavior bothered Dennis a lot. One day, years later, as adults, he talked to me about it. I discerned that the history aroused latent passion. Of what was said, this remark remained. "Leyland, of all the people in our neighborhood," "did you ever see anyone chasing and beating their children, or even flogging them like Daddy did?" My mind did a review of the then-known community. Dennis was absolutely right. He looked away and his mandibular muscles twitched.

Fear was always with me. It was the kind of fear that had no source; it had no form or place but kept me in a state of perpetual suspense—with no place of beginning and no relief. It was like what I've heard described as "butterflies in the stomach"—a free- floating thing warning of something impending. I did not eat well and often skipped lunch. I was skinny, obviously malnourished, and mostly withdrawn. According to Cecil, I looked "ribsy, like one of those Congolese children with bloated bellies." He was making a comparison to photographs of children caught in the Congo guerrilla war. I did well in school, but at exams, I preferred to be third or so in class. First place got me too much attention. Retrospectively, I can now identify how we were all scarred. No socially healthy home produces children with so many psychological pathologies. I attribute no blame to anyone.

Sister Carmen was beautiful and obedient, never asked for much, seemed content and was always jovial. She never seemed to be an initiator. Once, she was in a Christmas play and received a delightful, hard-covered storybook as an award for her schoolwork. We all loved to read it. When she finished primary school, there was nothing to elevate her. Her gendered options were very limited. So, she enrolled in a secretarial course at Mr. Yhipp's. It convened at five o'clock in the evening and lasted until about eight o'clock. The students were tutored in Pitman's shorthand and typewriting. Mr. Yhipp owned several typewriters and was known to be a good teacher. His class was well attended, even overcrowded, but I know of no graduate who benefited by a job with the Demerara Bauxite Company, the sole employer in the area for someone with those skills. After about a year or so, Mr. Yhipp's enterprise folded. However, it had no unfavorable effect on Carmen's life.

Dennis was always meticulously clean. I mean to say he was compulsively well groomed. The apple of our grandmother's eye, and my mother doted on him too. He was bright, but more self-obsessed than most people I know. Dennis' psychic defense mechanism for his underlying insecurity, perhaps anxiety, I believe, manifested as an inflated sense of self. He suffered a lot of emotional trauma. As a toddler, he was a head banger, a condition typical in severely neglected children. He butted the walls until one day his forehead encountered a nail. The scar from the injury remains, though it is now barely distinguishable.

Soon, Dennis developed a tic—in the form of an incessant blinking and squeezing of his eyes. He would compress the lids to the point where the insides of his eyelids peeled back, showing the pink tissue below. It worsened when he was anxious or agitated. His eyes teared for no apparent reason. It was not pretty, he also ground his teeth, thereby creating a kind of slow, screeching annoyance, not unlike scratching on a blackboard. When less stressed, he would clench his teeth such that an observer would witness long periods of twitching of his mandibular muscles. Dennis bit his nails frequently. He persisted until there was nothing left to nibble at but tiny pieces of dermal tissue the nails should have normally covered. Our mother thought he needed glasses, but no one got around to obtaining them.

Cecil, the more vigorous of my brothers, was always eager for a fight with Dennis. After having his way in the tumble Cecil usually received a torrent of multisyllabic responses and name-calling from Dennis. But for the most part, all was well with them. When they got to high school, their negative behaviors stopped, and they drew closer.

One day, with turmoil rife in the home and Dennis perceived to be favoring Mommy, there was an eruption. It was late afternoon. Daddy had just arrived from work and was sitting on the backstairs outside the kitchen morosely stewing, for reasons then unknown to me. I was in the yard cleaning some pipes for resale. Dennis, all sulky and snappish, relayed to Daddy a message from Mommy. Daddy asked for more information. Dennis, seemingly vexed, answered him offhandedly, whereupon Daddy, already irritated and now further angered, roughed him up in the backyard. He slapped Dennis about the head, chucked him, and then picked up a cinder block and threw it at him. I was aghast. The cinder block did not hit Dennis but landed near his feet after he dodged. It is possible that Daddy lowered his aim, given that their proximity gave the advantage to Daddy, and if he'd really wanted to hit him with the object he'd have likely succeeded. Whatever the case, Dennis stood cowed, sullen, and tearful. Though he said nothing, his eyes told me all.

Unbelievably, all of Dennis's symptoms ceased when he left home, thus confirming that the etiology might not have been organic. As to the glasses, he never needed them and was never again plagued by the supposed poor vision—if that is what it was.

For hyper-vigilant Cecil, my heart breaks. I do not believe that he had ever experienced deep, restful, refreshing, normal sleep. It's inexplicable how he managed to survive into adulthood. He evidenced classic indicators of food anxiety at about age twelve. He hoarded bread, despite having consumed his regular meals and lots of other food being available. A whole loaf would go missing at a time. Sometimes he would just take a few bites and fall asleep with the remains of the loaf in hand. When he could, he hid them in the ice cream churn or concealed them under his pillow or below his mattress or wherever else he thought they would be undetectable. In that compulsive state, he could not reason that only a very limited number of safe stashing spots were available in a small bedroom shared by four and cleaned by our mother and Carmen. Due to his condition, he could not have reasoned that, whenever bread was missing, Mommy or Carmen would go straight to him, since no one else in the home was stealing bread. With his normal reasoning impaired, it never occurred to him that, if a whole loaf was swiped, it was bound to be noticed. He only pilfered bread, not money or anything else. As to causation, rule out hunger, Interestingly, he would not go back and finish off his cache. This was a very disturbed child, hoarding for emotional security.

Cecil was inordinately fearful of the dark and anxious about being alone. I used to tell him long stories I would create as I went until he fell asleep between Dennis and me on a bed in the kitchen. Later, Cecil suffered frequent visual hallucinations, bed- wetting, talkativeness, argumentativeness, moderate stuttering, somnambulation, anxiety, and panic attacks. He also developed a habit of clicking his fingers at times while walking. If questioned on an issue, his explanation would eventually become so convoluted and interminable the other party would have to give up the issue. He would not go to the latrines alone by day or night and was afraid of the automatic flush. Sometimes on his pleadings, I would accompany him and stand near the doorway.

Every few minutes he would call to me and was, apparently, assured when I answered. He would keep talking and asked questions intermittently for confirmation of my presence. Poor guy. He was so impulsive and did not seem to be able to connect actions to consequences, imminent or distant. Cecil was always in trouble with our parents.

It was a Saturday afternoon, overcast and drizzling. There was this game we called raking, which was won by severing the opponent's string or rubber band. Only boys played raking; girls were too intelligent for that. Oh, no, I'm not biased! Which gender is known for going in a group to throw missiles at yellow jackets' nests, knowing beforehand what the unpleasant result will certainly be? Thank you.

The equipment, the raker, was simple to make; it cost nothing but time; and had an application that was, as you shall see, very dangerous. All that was needed was the bottom of a can and string or, if you had them, rubber bands. The can's round bottom was obtained by rubbing it on a concrete surface until the rim wore away. Done right, you end up with a thin, razor-sharp tin sphere into which two holes are punctured about a third of an inch apart. This was your "spinner" or "raker." What idle boy would not wish to have such a toy? Through the holes you loop the string or rubber band, and the plaything is ready for gaming. The shorter the string and sharper the spinner, the more formidable the instrument since the former increased its revolutions. With the strings looped around your thumbs, you were now ready to game. Think of an accordion. That's a good picture of the way your thumbs generate the spinning speed. As to the two holes, the closer to the center and the greater their proximity to each other, the more fear-inducing your spinner was.

The spinners made a low, threatening sound when in operation. As you worked the strings, the can bottom revolved forward and backward with a whoosh. Your goal was to go in on the opponent's string just as it is neared the limit of its expansion and make the cut. There was a little skill involved—timing, turning, going in crosswise, and such.

Teachers confiscated rakers on sight; adults constantly warned us of the dangers. But then we would congregate someplace else. Like my friends, I had a spinner, and so did Cecil.

There were two boys in the neighborhood most knew better than to challenge—or to accept their friendly invitation to a game. They were Clement and Compton, both of whom were skillful and daring. So, on this drizzly Saturday afternoon, a dozen boys had gathered below our stilted house. That was all the devil needed to do—just bring them together and they would soon concoct their own distress. I was a mere interested spectator. The brave, the reckless, and the stupid created contests, battled, voices low to avoid my mother's ears.

Then it happened just as the reader anticipated it would. Others having backed down, Cecil confidently accepted Compton's challenge. Friendly bets were made and the duel began in the midst of a tight circle of wide-eyed boys, their excited voices subdued.

Compton made short work of him. In a few seconds, Cecil's string was rived, but worse, his left thumb was sliced to the bone. The cut, inches long, extended onto the palm. I was appalled and worried for him—blood running everywhere and him trying feebly to stanch the flow. His pain, made worse by a sprinkling rain dripping into the gaping wound, was obvious.

Like Daddy's idiomatic parrot's bad company, the other boys all took speedy, silent flight in every direction. Strange, baffling it is how boys who, up to no good, know instinctively when it's running time. Without a word or hint of a signal, they instantaneously take off. They run, preferring the fastest; shortest; and, if possible, least visible route home, where they sit quietly, on their best behavior. Cecil stood, shocked, and confused, begging me not to tell Mommy. I asked how he planned to get healed, to which he replied that he would put some cobweb on it. He began seeking such remedy among the beams that supported our house.

However, he planned to conceal that serious an injury would certainly be absurd. I told him no and rushed to inform our mother. She looked out the window, called him, and exclaimed her horror when bloody Cecil reluctantly arrived nursing his left hand at the wrist with his right. Mommy, between dressing a customer's hair, dialed a taxi and telephoned Sister Stella at the hospital, asking her to expect Cecil. And off he went to the hospital, where he received an injection, eleven painful stitches, and a metal plate bandaged in place to immobilize his thumb. Daddy was doubly troubled, not simply because the expensive medical bills were to be deducted from his weekly paycheck but also because this was such a preventable expense.

Sometimes I muse about what I believe to be noteworthy coincidences in our family history. There are many. As we walk together through our story, the reader might have a little difficulty dismissing out of hand, the repetition of experiences and actions I connect. Similarities and disparities will be explained a bit later. For the moment, I'll leap ahead briefly and tell a little of my father's own mistreatment, the disclosure of which, at this time, might give context to what I'm ready to say.

My father, then little Albert, suffered the indignity of being an unwanted child. One day, enraged over Albert's trifling transgression, my grandfather seized him and inflicted a terrible cut across his left palm. It was a long, deep cut, extending from his left thumb, through his soft palm.

Cecil's injury was the same place on the body as was Daddy's; both were just as severe, and each was inflicted by someone else. The consequential difference—Cecil's father immediately provided him emergency medical care by competent professionals in a hospital setting.

CHAPTER V

BROKEN CHILDREN, BROKEN PARENTS, BROKEN CHILDREN

AN EMOTIONALLY UNSTABLE home, combined with authoritarian parenting, produces emotionally insecure children. The children live in a world of uncertainty, ambiguity, tension, generalized fear, and unpredictability. I suffered an eating disorder, listlessness, compulsivity, regressive behaviors, social anxiety, and unusual vigilance. With no insight about the nature of my psychological condition, my parents opted for the well-known "solutions"— (1) ignore it or (2) beat it out of him, unsparingly. The combination and complexities of our domestic situation led, I believe, to my experiences of colorful, disturbing, dreams. I was a psychic wreck who managed to con everyone into believing he was highly disciplined and absolutely dependable. Beware, beware the fellow who is always on time.

Nothing happens absent a reason. That is a fact. It is also true that behaviors occur contextually and that specific triggers may provoke certain responses. These statements can all be supported empirically.

A cursory literature review informs us that, though we can construct models, scales, and so on with sophistry, we cannot conclude that certain stimuli applied to given situations will cause every human being to respond identically every time, even to pain. So, we rely on criteria, conduct statistical analyses, create benchmarks and scales, and study patterns and clusters to help us understand why some individuals or groups act the way they do. At minimum, we know that certain traits predispose subjects, all things being equal, to adopt certain attitudes, and we know how those attitudes may or may not impinge on interactions within families.

Social scientists have managed to classify parenting into two general types—authoritarian and permissive. We may look at Daddy's parenting (his father's, past actions and, from a cluster of behavioral hints on both, conclude that both of these men's parenting styles were profoundly authoritarian. This should surprise no objective thinker, given that they were both raised in a task-oriented plantocracy, where absolute obedience and docility were preferred values—these demands being necessary to maintain tranquility and productivity. The character Boxer in George Orwell's Animal Farm would be easily outmatched in loyal servitude.

In an authoritarian-parented household, a professional would expect to find extremes in certain attitudes and behaviors, including:

(1) Inflexible, "black or white" thinking exhibited by the dominant parent ("You're either for me or against me")
(2) Rigid rules external to the self
(3) A tendency toward obsessive reliance on discipline
(4) The equation of discipline with punishment
(5) High value placed on vague, capricious order
(6) A view of obedience as the highest value
(7) Mandatory group loyalty
(8) Extreme conformity
(9) Poor conflict resolution capabilities
(10) Inability to readily express feelings and choices
(11) The fostering of an external locus of control
(12) The perception of internal development and independent decision making threatens the authority figure.

The authoritarian perceives himself or herself as weak; believes he or she is the source of any problem; and believes problems must be solved by constant, incrementally harsh punishment. Soon the family is dysfunctional, trapped in cycles of absolute violence and rebelliousness. The parents and children form coalitions, sub- groups forced into alignment. In such a fissured family, secrets pervade, and perception is reality. The powerful parent blames the subordinate other and expands the circle of abuse to her or him. This degenerates, more often than not, to the more authoritarian parent managing and bullying the family. There, we may find referrals for discipline. For example, the mother might declare to a misbehaving child, "Just you wait till your father gets home. You know what will happen then!"

In terms of alignment, let's look at the example of that episode of Dennis taking a message to his father, sent by his mother. She could not have been more than forty feet away. Examined, it may be accurate to conclude that the parents were not speaking to each other. Communication between the adults was then facilitated by the child, sympathetic to his mother. Was Daddy's physical attack on Dennis due to Dennis's flippancy? If we concede that, we are still to consider the hitting in terms of appropriateness and proportionality. Fist-beating your child in public indicates much more than disregard for your son and a lack of parental self-respect.

It is a grave mistake to try to label parents as good, bad, or whatever tag one wishes to use. The discovery surprising to some, is that these parents do love their children, just as the children love their parents. Often, the parents are reacting with what they know, and they themselves wish their situation would get better. Not knowing what to do is not a sin.

Some noteworthy behaviors in such a home might include:

(a) Fixed adherence to conventional rules and competition to please
(b) Fearful subservience to parental demands
(c) Unwillingness to tolerate ambiguity
(d) Abuse of power as acceptable and normalized
(e) Verbal threats of violence, bullying, scapegoating, and aggressive parental shaming as normative
(f) Presence of extreme physical aggression

My mother must have been very ambivalent about me. Her recurrent annoyance with me was often verbalized as "you ugly, flat-faced bitch." She sometimes described me; yelled at me and would slap me in the face hard, and her ring hurt as much as the scorn. One night, from across the kitchen, she threw an empty can, striking me on the left side of my head inflicting a cut on my scalp. It bled. She laughed while managing insincere contriteness, saying only that she did not know it would cut me. What was notable was that she hit me with the can for the amusement of the family sitting about, not for anything I had done.

On the other hand, she was loving and protective of me. But for her pleas and protestations to my father that he should not hit me "so hard," he might have broken my neck. There was truly that possibility. His hitting could be precipitated by something as trifling as my not having gone with sufficient immediacy on an errand or, if I was hurrying, then it's not showing happiness to go. If I hurried and showed eagerness, my father had a hatbox full of unlimited possible reasons to justify an attack. Sometimes as I passed him, Daddy would reach out with a sudden blow to the back of my head or nape of my neck. Inevitably, I would fall to the ground, and my mother would intercede. She would always be the one to quickly pick me up from the floor. Cecil sulked his disapproval, but he couldn't do anything preventive. I assumed that other siblings thought his bullying, abusive behavior was normal discipline. Sad to say, he sometimes did it simply for their amusement. Carmen used to exclaim "pow" as she laughed. She was not a malicious person thus I am dumfounded as to why she found the episodes mirthful. It only encouraged him.

It might be true to report that, due to the way our family was split, I had no real role, or chore, so to speak. At times, I was treated as the oldest boy among the younger subset, and other times, I'd be given "female" tasks. So in this duality of expectations, any chore could be mine, at any time. From going to the market for meat, bread, and greens and other perishables to doing the weekly grocery shopping from Cho Kang or other merchants, to going to buy some hair nets, to carrying a message, to going to pick up some razor blades, to taking this box hand (sous) to Miss X. The latter refers to weekly pooling small amounts of money taking turns collecting. Sous is based on absolute trust. It seemed to be a constant Go, Go, Go! My time was never my own. The unpredictability and urgency were so frustrating.

One Saturday morning, I had just had it! This is an instance that confirmed for me that Cecil had difficulty in linking actions to consequences in a logical way. I believe that to be his undiscovered impairment. He was intellectually able in every other way, but undoubtedly, he had a blind spot.

It began when Mommy told me to cut the grass at the front and the side of the house. Sour and hungry, watching the tropical sun move well into it's midmorning position, and having just unwillingly completed some other task, I was beside myself with suppressed rage turned inward. Cecil, standing beside my path toward the front yard, eyed me curiously as I strode with the weighty cutlass to begin weeding.

"What's wrong?" he asked casually, despite my very obvious distress.

In anger I blurted, "They're working me too hard. Sometimes I just feel like killing myself."

I was merely venting, maybe, but Cecil, now standing nearby, heard me and got more interested. He crept closer.

"Do you really want to kill yourself"? Cecil asked, quietly, while appraising me sidewise.

"Yes, I do." I said in plaintive exasperation.

"How would you do it?" Cecil pressed with a measured tone and patience.

"I would hang myself, and then I wouldn't have to bother with all this, all the time," I cried dispiritedly.

I was by now palpably furious and frustrated to tears. Cecil subtly goaded in a manner disguised as reasoning. "Well there's no rope, so without a rope, you can't do it, right? I mean how can you hang yourself without a rope?" He paused in feigned reflection and went in search of some suitable instrument for my undoing, rummaging among some junk nearby.

On his return, he looked about quickly and then added, "Well, there's this dog chain ... but ..." He pretended to dismiss an unspoken alternative nonchalantly. "Ah, I bet you won't do it, anyway," he reproached as he carelessly swung the chain between us, waiting, waiting, timing, now, pretending to be uninterested.

Weirdly, by now I was buck wild, so highly motivated, just about to seek possession of the chain while begging for the opportunity to kill myself. "Yes, I will. You watch." I insisted, having been skillfully manipulated into a Faustian choice by my older brother. Of course, now I had to be bolder and more resolute than ever. My options were simple: (1) hang your miserable, disgruntled little self and be done with it or, (2) be a proven coward—worse, maybe even a sissy boy. Of course! Of course, I chose hanging. What else was a man to do? The options were either-or, and the question close-ended. That was it.

"Okay then," he said with upward inflection, badly suppressing any hint of excitement. "Let's see if you really would do it."

Thereupon I climbed onto the backrest of our yard bench as Cecil had suggested. It was shaky due to the unevenness of the ground. But that was solved by Cecil offering to hold the bench steady as I mounted. Smiling, he secured the dog chain to a metal bracket above, and we both put the chain around my neck, fitting it close.

The unforgiving dog chain secured, Cecil then stepped back and yelled, "Yaagh!" intending to startle me. Simultaneously he shook the bench. I lost my footing on the backrest, and suddenly, I was suspended and being strangled. Me, me?! I remember feeling the flush of blood building in my head, my hearing abuzz, my heart pounding in my ear. My skinny neck stiffened reflexively, all tendons strained, and I could not speak. I dangled, choked, and kicked but things were, unfortunately, going just as we had planned. Everything was blurred. My hands holding the chain, I tried to pull myself up. I remember my legs flailing about, trying to recover my footing. Unbelievable! How could this be? I was being hanged. I was indeed being hanged!

As Dennis rounded the curb, he immediately grasped the situation's urgency. His propitious arrival on a bicycle and his better judgment prevented further constriction of my neck. He raised an alarm from the road, shouting, "Hey, hey, what y'all doing?" Then he repeated that even louder—his voice indicating grave, urgent concern. Cecil helped me down. My mother, having heard Dennis's alarm, came running from within the house, arriving incredulous at her two sons' unmitigated stupidity. My life was saved.

When a woman has six children, a few of them crazy, she is condemned to run. There is always some emergency. Thus, she is always "ready-set," prepared to go remedy the next crisis. She would have been running a few weeks later when, playing with fire, I lit a floorcloth that was set out drying against the kitchen wall. I might have burned the house down, but I managed to douse that flame in three trips to the kitchen sink, without anyone knowing.

Questioned by Mommy about the near-death calamity, Cecil explained, "It wasn't me. He wanted to do it."

His response was so innocent and matter of fact that, looking back, I see again a good brother who seemed to constantly be in search of risk. One would think I should then have been wary of him, but oh, no. Such is the influential power of a big brother.

On that Saturday morning I resolved sternly not to attempt hanging myself again, with or without assistance.

One night, Cecil thought it a good idea for us to go to the community pool so he could teach me to swim. Little did I know that he could barely swim. I knew that his high school offered pool and gym classes, but I never saw him actually swim. I wanted to learn, and he desired to teach—better seize the opportunity.

It was a little before eight o'clock and dark. We slipped out of the house unnoticed by our parents, walked through the backyard onto Berbice Road, and then completed the short trek along Greenheart Street to the community swimming pool. There were no lights about the premises, though the pool was slightly illuminated by the sports club nearby, where a game of football was in progress. Full of vim and vigor, we scampered across the modest lawn undetected, had no trouble scaling the picket fence, undressed to our briefs, used the ladder, and quickly entered the cool water. I shivered. At the west end, the shallow end that is, I was able to stand, but frightened by my buoyancy, I held tight to the gutter that formed the perimeter of the pool's walls, worried that, should I slip, I would be immediately submerged and incapable of regaining a perpendicular position. But that concerned me less than not knowing how to swim. Plus, I had a confident big brother instructing me. What on earth could go wrong?

Cecil taught his first lesson, which consisted of instructing me to kick while holding onto the concrete gutter. That session lasted less than two minutes, and then off we were toward the middle of the pool, Cecil leading me by the hand. He supported me in the water while I did as told, that being to paddle and kick. A few seconds later, he withdrew his hands, his crazy expectation being that I would start swimming off. It was the moment all hell broke loose in the dark pool. I went under headfirst, swallowing my way to the bottom, arms and legs flailing. Deafening bubbles took over my ears, and my eyes burned. I could not tell which side was up; it seemed like I was cartwheeling with no control. Like any normal person in a similar predicament, I inhaled as much water as possible and drank more in huge gulps. Then more! This wasn't working as expected. The chlorine burned my eyes and seared my nostrils. Yes, I was in deep—really deep—and I was disoriented, too wild to be afraid.

I remember a sensation similar to observing oneself under water. I tumbled and rotated. Instinctively, I grabbed about for Cecil but was unable to grasp him. All I knew was water and lots of big, noisy bubbles. Confusion!

"Stand up! Stand up!" Cecil's voice was urgent, but where it came from I did not know.

Water and bubbles. Huge gulps of choking, chlorinated water. I locked onto Cecil's neck, and he desperately tried to pull free.

"Yes, you can stand up. This is the shallow side. Stand up! Stand up! I heard Cecil but still had no idea where exactly he was. Then I realized he was holding my shoulders, shaking me. I hauled in the deepest, loudest, sweetest breath I have ever known. This had not gone quite as expected for either of us.

Now sufficiently chastened and scared witless, we began exiting the pool the way we'd come. Only this time we were not nimble but glum. This had all happened within minutes of our descent into the water. Both of us looked like we had encountered a raging tiger with cubs. I was filled with chlorinated water, eyes, and nostrils still afire, and all interest in swimming had been shaken from my shuddering body.

We said nothing until we were well on the way along Greenheart Street heading home, as mischievous boys are known to do. Who needed to learn to swim anyway?!

Cecil broke the silence with a question. "Why you so stupid?" he asked, rhetorically.

I didn't answer.

"Man, I was telling you that all you had to do was just stand up—simple as that. But you gone and start panicking," said Cecil, once we were on the road, his confidence now returning.

"What you panicking for?" he continued, seeking no answer.

Now, I suspected that he was as terrified as I but trying to conceal his own awesome fright by directing anger toward me.

"I felt I was drowning," I countered.

Cecil adopted the mien of a teacher to a grade school student who just won't get it. For him it was all so elementary. "Look, man, I tell you, all you had to do was kick and paddle, just kick and paddle," he said with a tsk and hint of frustration. "You can't drown in the shallow side," he added, distinctly articulating each word, "You can't drown in the shallow side."

He was trying to convince me of what I knew was not true. Gracious, I had just experienced it. I do hope that he doesn't believe that still.

And yep, that was the night I sternly resolved never to drown myself with or without assistance. The feeling of complete submersion and helplessness is much too much to swallow.

Troubled boys head home. That we did.

Cecil and I came very close to drowning that night all in the space of less than five minutes of his tutelage. Guess we would have been in big trouble with our parents if we had died that night—and mostly because we had snuck out of the house.

Cecil never got a third chance to recklessly mislead me, though another time I did agree to allow him to practice barbering on my head. He convinced me that he had been taught by our respected friend, Morris. I was skeptical, but I knew Morris did backyard haircuts using only a comb and razor blade. Would this end well? Oh, no! We gave up about five minutes into that. Continuing would have been a bloodbath—a slow death, the result of a nip here, a nick there, now, and then a pinch, a big chunk of my ear eventually being caught between the scissors' blades—another adventure with Cecil gone terribly wrong.

CHAPTER VI

SPARE THE ROD, LOVE THE CHILD

I SHALL ALWAYS remember the last caning I got from my father. It is indelible, not only for its ferocity, duration, and unjustness, but because that one moment clarified and confirmed for me my supposition that I was least wanted. I cannot help describing this occurrence as manifestly indicative of what might have pushed me from Daddy and, as we shall see, supplied the kindling for the combustion that was destined. It was punishment for so insignificant a transgression, that but for the violence, it would not have even been remembered. In fact, it could not have been a transgression since no rule had been broken. Walk with me in the slight divergence. The incident would be best understood in context.

I moved from first standard to third standard and continued doing fine in fourth. I think my exceptional progress was lost, unnoticed by our family since no one commented on it. I continued to excel—that is, until some well-intentioned bureaucrat's creative mind decided that the school needed to select a few promising pupils for a scholarship class when the term was already well under way. I was one of the chosen four children.

Unfortunately, the decision to move me, then a skinny, constantly hungry kid, to the scholarship class with no preparation was bad and its execution, worse. No one asked my parents. It was left to me to tell them.

Out of place and disconnected from the older kids, I passed most of the day in a stupor. Then it happened—the students' bane. Dictation! The pace was faster than I was accustomed and the words unfamiliar. I got twenty-one errors.

That night was the only time I remember either parent going over my homework. That was because someone must have told them. It could not have come from the school since communication between our parents and school was non-existent. I guess it was one of my siblings who just happened to see the numerous red lines, informed them. "What! Twenty-one errors"! Exclaimed my mother. There then ensued a chorus of what I needed to do and that I played too much. You know how it goes. That was nothing compared to what was to come.

About a week or so later, a teacher, Mr. Banke, offered tutoring on Saturday mornings at nine o'clock. It was not compulsory, and only a few students went. I, like many others, chose not to go. The whole family was sitting around in light chat, the mood fine, when Sister Carmen noticed about three children going to the lessons, mentioned it, and my absolute horror became a living, breathing thing.

My father, dresses in a pair of cream shorts and white singlet, approached spritely—not a question asked, no explanation given, no supplication heeded. He seemed glad for an opportunity to teach me a lesson. His immediate purposefulness forewarned that this was not an admonition or just a spanking in the making. My father, rashly angered to a fit, sprang on me with a cane and began a blind drubbing the likes of which I had never ever seen, much less suffered. That I shall never forget. I cannot forget. It isn't that I harbor no anger or bitterness, but the profound unjustness and ferocity make it impossible for me to forget. It was like an attack premeditated, seeking only the flimsiest a reason for justification. I had never been struck so hard, for so long and so many times in my life. It would not stop. He rained blows incessantly, unfeeling, uncaring where I was struck. In retreat, I fell backward down the kitchen stairs, screaming. Now upside down, both arms needed for instinctive self-protection, I could not get upright. It appeared he took advantage of that. He just would not cease. He stood over me and beat and beat, the cane raining its way down from his towering position on the upper step. And no one said stop. No one dared, merely to say, okay Daddy, he's had enough. No, I was on my own without a white knight.

That was when it happened. It was precisely at that moment that it, hard to describe to one who has never experienced it, the captured snapshot came—a split second when all seems to slow and stop. In this fraction of time and mind unsynchronized, the blows no longer felt, that the revelation occurred. I looked up into his narrowed, blazing eyes. How brown they were, I thought; I'd never noticed that before, so light it was like gold. There I was marveling at the color of my father's eyes in the midst of my own victimization. But there, in those eyes, I perceived a loathing—a contempt so real and deep it remains vivid to this day. I had let loose his suppressed, unmerciful, insensate hatred. But was it me? Was I the object? I had never done him anything wrong, never rude to either parent. What was I really dealing with? Well, we cannot ever know.

That was certainly the instant where our new relationship was clearly defined, the old derailed and the new begun. As the others' actions evinced, everyone in the house felt bad about what had occurred. I knew that because, after it was over, they all settled into awkward silence. Some looked someplace else; others went out the back or the front door. It was like a contagion had arrived suddenly, all family members moving away from each other, none toward me, and none toward him. Only the snapshot abided me.

I believe that there is a tenuous, trusting, consanguinity between fathers and sons that, once violated, seems very hard to mend—their established bond irretrievable. Nothing new here; the literature of antiquity is full of references to father-son relationships.

For us, love and paternal tenderness were replaced with obligatory maintenance and unwavering duty to each other. Per Shakespeare, when love begins to sicken and decay, it useth an enforced ceremony.

The class was discontinued after only that singular session. But our bridge had already been seriously damaged.

The moment is forgiven. I wish it could be forgotten. But even time has not diminished that chiseled image.

I thought it best to inform the reader early on what discipline was like in our home and how the ambivalence to it, at least in part, may have contributed to the behaviors, feelings, and relationships there. We all coped differently, and the lives of each of us, parents, and children, were affected diversely, some of us adversely.

I tried to be as honest and revealing about what happened and the possible contributors to the situation. I do not know the reason my father beat me like that. I request of my reader not to be too hurried to interpret my father's harshness as described, to mean he was a bad parent (however that is defined, I don't pretend to know). That merely simplifies him. A true conclusion remains usefully elusive. That was only a part of his being and does not demean or establish his whole character. He was, undoubtedly abusive, very much so, but interpreted and compared to my father's childhood, with an appreciation of intergenerational transmissions of values and behaviors, he did just what he knew. He was a devoted father, an unfailing provider. He tried his best, and I miss hearing him say, "Come, come, Brods."

It didn't end there. It seems it never does. One of my most precious memories happened after my late wife and I had our two children. When the kids were about three and five, their mother would dress them, and they wait on the bridge to our house. The first one to see me take the turn home would start running to meet me. The two would run as fast as they could, their smiles broad, their eyes flickering their joy. When we met, I would dismount my bicycle and then put one on the pedals and the other on the carriage and roll them all the way home. They would be so happy it broke my heart. We were so melded that other relatives felt I spoiled them. I was never one to favor physical discipline of children.

After migrating to the United States, there was a tremendous amount of pressure on me; in fact, we all felt it, if variety is considered. Holding two full-time jobs while "catching your hand" on weekends, meant that for me everything had to be scheduled. Regimented might be an apt expression. When you eat, when you shower, when you get Mariel from school, when you sleep—everything had to be coordinated to detail. The busses and trains were running my life, and I was complicit in ruining my life. Like my father, I was a dependable provider. I was not a husband, friend, or father, so slavish was I. The "either-or thinking" of the authoritarian insidiously crept in. The stress wore me to the point where medical help was imperative.

At one session I self-reported to my therapist that I had slapped my children, Fiona, and Marvin, in the face.

He, my therapist, quickly got very serious and silent. In the long pause, he scrutinized me, his gaze empathetic, his eyes penetrating, and then asked in an even tone, "Have you ever done that before?"

"No." My anguished reply escaped me. Flustered, I added, looking again at the familiar office carpet, "I am said to be too permissive with the kids—that I spoil them."

"Don't do it again," he advised. I assured him I wouldn't.

He sat quietly, looking deep within me. "When nothing else seems to be working, parents return to what worked in humans' primal state … We hit," said my therapist.

"Do you think it will happen again?" he queried, unobtrusively. I whispered, "No," shaking my contrite head.

"I didn't think so," he said and smiled.

My therapist tilted backward a little in his chair. After another long pause came his disarming question, so incisive and clear, so insightful. "Mr. King, who do you really want to hit?"

I didn't answer. None was needed. He smiled his empathy. He already knew that I knew.

My therapist looked at me compassionately and said slowly, "Mr. King, if your children only knew what you go through, if they only knew".

Like the brilliance of a cloudless summer noon, I realized that I was beginning to live my father's life, as he had his father's. I was witnessing the disintegration of my second family. I could not discern which was worse, the feeling of powerlessness or the deepening hopelessness. I knew I was becoming my father, and that I found intolerable.

'Not so cocky now, are yah?' my devilish, judgmental side sneered, mocking, and relishing my heartbreak.

The probable cause of dysfunction known, I soon found the solution, and my determination at once kicked in. I went home, got out my notebook, and methodically constructed a five-year plan with specific goals, concrete steps, and milestones. *Some crucial choices must be made and shall be, I determined. I am in charge of only one person, me.*

CHAPTER VII

Carrying the Baton, Completing the Relay

IN 1967, STANLEY KRAMER produced the popular movie Guess Who's Coming to Dinner. It was a story of the storms surrounding interracial marriage in the United States, the resistance of prospective in-laws and the conflict the lovers have with their own parents. Though the plot was much like that of Romeo and Juliet, West Side Story, and others of that genre, it was pretty courageous to make that movie when bigotry and social change were tearing the country apart.

For me and my friends, the most interesting, memorable scene was the confrontational dialogue between John, a doctor, and his father, Roy, who, furiously opposed the union. Roy asked his son if the marriage outside of his race was the way he would repay the twenty-seven thousand miles he'd carried a mailbag to give him the best opportunities and the fact that his wife had done without, sacrificing necessities for her son. John retorted angrily, "I owe you nothing. You were doing what you were supposed to do as your duty as a father. I do not care if you carried that bag a million miles. When my son comes along, I have to do the same for him."

Adolescence being what it is, my friends and I talked about it a lot. Daddy saw this movie too, but we never discussed it. Apart from the angelic flawlessness of the young doctor, quite right in his supposition and quite wrong in "handling" his father, this is what got lost in the confrontation and ought to be remembered: There are moral and legal expectations about the father's duty to provide protection; sustenance; emotional, material, and educational supports to his child. But there are no qualitative rules about the father's duty to his child. Neither parent, for that matter, has to provide salmon over catfish, an Ivy League university over community college, and certainly not designer clothes and showy accoutrements over thrift-store hand-me-downs. In divorce proceedings, no spouse is morally entitled to ten thousand dollars a week in child support just because the other spouse is rich— the specious argument being that such was the child's standard of living he or she was accustomed to. Really? Love and duty, though compatible, are distinctly dissimilar. Blessed are parents who honor both.

Just as parents' duty to their children is unequivocal, enduring, and universal, so too is the duty of children to their parents and grandparents. One has also duties to brothers and sisters and to aid aunts, uncles, and so on. The values are grounded in survival, but they may also be intrinsic. Expediency makes its own case. Social institutions and scriptural, moral, and ethical philosophy all expound these values and encourage reciprocal ties and altruistic behaviors, strong and tight in the core family and becoming more nebulous as the distance in kinship recedes. But even then, the bond to all life is still strong through empathic, altruistic, and spiritual concerns.

The society based on "rugged individualism" never was. "Survival of the fittest", has to do with genetic selection, not how much an individual can grab and gorge himself. Please unlearn the meme propagated by an insatiable, greedy, selfish class of people to justify theft and plunder of public wealth. I daresay, it never can be because of three very basic issues we cannot get around. If we could, by now, we would have.

First, the more technologically advanced we become, the more we have to depend on specialists for our very existence. Guess the recluse with a smartphone high in a mountain's cave or in a penthouse reaching for the clouds are as unimaginable to you as they are confounding to me. Siri is a poor, indifferent companion; finicky too. Certain things she just will not do.

The second reason is regeneration of the species and bonding. A human newborn, though remarkably resilient, is difficult to keep alive, teach, and raise to maturity. It's tough out there.

Thirdly, we have physiological and psychological needs for affiliation and love. Being social beings is one of the main reasons we stay at the top of the food chain and able to communicate instantaneously around the world.

The fact that, after thousands of years of human evolution, the basics of social needs and organization persist, make its own case. That said, let's take a look at this exchange that took place on September 16, 2104, between an anonymous user and myself on

TUMBLER: destroy the idea that biological families are more valid than other forms of family. destroy the idea that your parents/siblings/extended relatives have an inherent right to be a part of your life if you don't want them to be.

TODDLER THE TERRIBLE: Seems to me that any of us can make that personal decision at any moment we choose. Others have in the past. Whatever your beliefs, secular or religious, history is full of examples like the prodigal son. Reciprocity is non- binding in many relationships. I am just curious as to when is the best age to sever these ties? By age 3, 5, 18? How about age 72? Just want to be sure when, exactly, commitments to family should end.

To live free of connectedness, rejecting interdependence is to choose a life of incessant, cognitive jujitsu and bold self-deception. Conscience's unrelenting offensive is never vanquished, its gnawing torment never assuaged. If that's not sufficient to convince one, then consider the matter of the diminished odds of a fruitful life. That is not a desirable existence and is an unnecessarily high price to pay for one's pursuit of strict self-interest and individualism. Surely, most of us would be miserable but for the support, material and psychological, of loyal kin. Our assistance in alleviating suffering of less prosperous relatives and friends is life affirming. A settled issue it is that humans are unable to fully care for themselves from birth through pre-adolescence, and again when sick, old, or infirm. Oh yes, and when they are in trouble. The mythical Sphinx must have observed our neediness well, leading her to formulate the famed riddle posed to the misfortunate many and finally to Oedipus himself:

"Creature walks on four legs in the morning, two at noon and three in the evening".

Though there are many interpretations of the riddle and inserted various solutions, the answer, man, I believe to be the most popular and reasonable. Some scholars assert the meaning to be the three stages of Oedipus' arrogant, egotistical, incestuous life, culminating with his tragic, self-inflicted helplessness and loss of those he loved, may disappoint some, we have to trust and depend on others much more than our pigheaded pride allows us to admit; and we will much, much more in the future—as the writer, soi-disant philosopher, and dauntless proponent of Individualism, Ayn Rand, ignominiously experienced when aged and indigent in a government-funded institution she so reviled in her better days, now accepting welfare checks, the curtains descending on her selfish life's ultimate act.

CHAPTER VIII

LIFE'S ROTATING WHEEL

As you do for your ancestors, your children will do for you.
— AFRICAN PROVERB

TWENTY YEARS IN child protective investigations and thirteen years as a police officer have led me to believe there are no perfect families, but there are numerous families who, over time and patient practice, have improved their adroitness at concealment of the unflattering and distracting attention to highlight the praiseworthy. Perhaps that's how unearned respect is granted.

This might be the opportune moment to bring forward a part of my family's history of which no one is proud. Just like any other family, we do have those parts. It is an account of what can happen when values of filial love, loyalty, and duty are discounted; one lives for the present and the satisfaction principally of one's self. At some time comes the cold dawn's awakening truth that what goes around, with certitude, does come around.

When Daddy was first introduced to Mommy's mother, Adelaide, she did not care to know him. Worse still, she disparaged him "there and then" as we say. He memorialized the event, refreshing it by repetition to us every now and then. Throughout his life, he avoided his mother-in-law's company when he was able, and she contributed little that counterbalanced her regrettable offense. It is fair to say that, to hold a singular error in one's unforgiving heart, one has to, of necessity, disregard or, at the very least, minimize, every good and generous act the offending person has done—as did my father the acts his mother-in-law did for us over the years. Her one mistake thus became, in my father's eyes, the totality of her character.

However, Mommy's grandmother (Maa-ma) took a liking to him. In a disagreement, Daddy could count on her to be his champion, confidant, and counselor. Maa-ma lived ninety-two years. Her daughter, Adelaide (Mommy's mother) paid her scant attention and reportedly had her needlessly institutionalized at the Alms House on Brickdam, Georgetown. Mommy was disconcerted by what she deemed to be Adelaide's carelessness and dispatch, when asked by medical staff if they should continue providing treatment. Adelaide, her nearest kin, allegedly signed a consenting document of some kind, and Maa-ma passed away. Just as Adelaide did not offer love and care for Mommy (Mommy was raised by her paternal great-aunt), it appears that there was no loving bond between the maternal elders. Mommy often talked about it, but it might have been only a matter of perception. We'll never know precisely that shadowed part of our history.

But what we do know, with absolute certainty is that Mommy, in turn, placed Adelaide in the same institution, where she expired a few years later. Her road to the home for the old and indigent was long and meandering, tempting and taunted by the what- ifs of regret. The bitter walk was slow and unwilling, but she arrived eventually and died there alone, as her mother, our great-grandmother, had.

Hold my hand and accompany me back a lifetime. It is important for the reader to connect the circumstances of Adelaide's demise to choices she might have thought best earlier in her life. Adelaide never worked outside the home, not that uncommon at the time. She was content to live unmarried to Uncle Eddie, who hailed from West Berbice. A stocky, taciturn man, he walked with a sway instead of a swagger. Observing him on his way home with his lunch bag, one might be tempted to think him a sailor. A closer look would quickly dispel that notion. The discerning eye would soon detect that he was lurching that way and this because his weight was poorly distributed and he was slightly knock-kneed. His middle was a weighty mass carried by chubby thighs. When sitting, shirtless and relaxed at the top of his back stairs, enjoying an evening's breeze, Uncle Eddie reminded one of popular images of the Buddha, so complacent, good-natured, and tubby he appeared. He was a strong man, a well-paid railroad laborer, employed by Demerara Bauxite Company, an expatriate industrial enterprise and Alcan subsidiary. We called him Uncle Eddie as a show of respect. He mispronounced my name all his life, but I liked him in an unexpressive way. He spoke little but was always nice to me. I never heard him raise his voice in anger or be haughty with anyone.

This is not a judgment of their choice not to marry; that was their prerogative. The wisdom of marriage could be contested from several perspectives since one might be just as happy or unhappy whether married or not. One may raise children, whether related to them or not. In this particular case, though, the decision to remain unwed could not have been a carefully studied one. Well, so it seemed.

Matrimony is codified, and many benefits accrue, favoring surviving kin; responsibilities too are delineated. Equally important, it governs the orderly and final transfer of bequeathed wealth. Real and intangible personal estate, future benefits, compensation for accidental death, and order of legal standing are all lost if the living arrangement is merely cohabitant, and the decedent left no will.

The duration of time the faithful couple shared home and bed is immaterial to the probate court.

Uncle Eddie was a simple, amiable fellow. He shunned close friendships; had no detectable vices or deep interests; was just barely literate; could not ride a bicycle; never learned to dance; and, though exceptionally superstitious, never knew a pew. His routine was to leave for work about 6:00 a.m. and return about 4:00 p.m., never once missing the train either way. I never heard of him absenting work or being sick. He appeared happiest at dinnertime, when he would scarf down an enormous quantity of food from a small basin on his back stairway and, once satiated, release sonorous belches without the slightest embarrassment or apology.

Uncle Eddie went to the movies once. It was to see Quo Vadis in colorful CinemaScope. He enjoyed it so much that he excitedly related to me what he thought to be the most exciting part. So impressed was he that, without being asked, he happily gave me money to go see it. I appreciated that and thanked him.

One Easter, while I was temporarily residing with Uncle Eddie made me a kite. It was small, simple, and papered in green and white. The frame, made of dried palm spine held together by a common pin. He constructed a nose because it was a "boy kite" and expected it to sing. I loved it more than any other kite I ever had. He had carefully made it just for me, unasked, string to knotted tail. In the bright sunshine of an Easter day, Uncle Eddie helped me raise it and stayed with me for hours, sitting in an open, grassy field. He spoke little but a genuine smile brightened his countenance, and clearly, he was enjoying the only outing we ever had. That kite sang, flew, and danced the southwestern sky for hours, and Uncle Eddie evinced benevolent satisfaction. Yes, he was unmistakably happy, and I was happy too. The string snapped in the late afternoon. My beloved kite drifted, waved, spun and flapped; then it slowly descended to some far unknown place, where finally the wind would desert it.

Daddy regarded Uncle Eddie with nominal respect. Both Daddy and Mommy thought him miserly and joked about the extremes he would suffer to save a penny. Ah, but Uncle Eddie built a house at Wismar and titled it to himself. He owed no one. All this accomplished in just a few years by a man poor in education and enormously rich in self-mastery. Sad to say, his distrust for banks and saving societies led him to cache his money in wads of large bills, secured by rubber bands. The coils were cleverly concealed in separate places, like his never-used leather shoes, placed under his bed. Some he secured in the pockets of a couple of suits he never wore and had no occasion to wear. For over twenty years he, by choice, and Adelaide, supposedly by codependency, lived unnecessarily sparing lives. Grandmother Adelaide had no minor children at the time. Her two adult children, Elaine, my mother and her younger brother, Kenneth were of two different fathers. We never met either of them. There will be more on this later. Uncle Eddie never had a child. With sufficiency of income, a good pension for later life, the couple had no need to squirrel away coins like Silas Marner.

One morning when Eddie was at work laying railroad track, a laden crane swayed and tilted ominously. Nearby workers shouted alarm while fleeing the danger. Uncle Eddie ran too but tripped and fell in the path of the crane's descent. The boom crushed his back. News spread quickly.

On hearing of the accident Adelaide rushed to get to the hospital. The ambulance bearing the fifty-three-year-old, mortally wounded Uncle Eddie sped past her on Parsons Road to the hospital about two miles away. Taking advantage of her confusion, Adelaide's trusted neighbors and friends looted the couple's precious stash. As if that were not sufficient grief for Adelaide, both her partner and their savings gone and unrecoverable, worse was yet to come.

His wake was ordinary—all lights on, door and windows open throughout the night, hymns sung and Psalms read into the wee hours with a little rum for the ancestral spirits. Crackers and coffee served, along with plantains and cassava sliced lengthwise and cooked in coconut milk. Concurrent with that event, his coffin was being built at the house diagonally across the street from ours. As usual, the carpenters hammered, screwed, and polished late into the night.

The company launch christened "Polaris," a sleek, white, modern vessel noted for its soft throb, speed, and sharp prow, was available to convey the bereaved and the lately deceased to Christiansburg Cemetery a few miles downriver. There, after a simple graveside ceremony, Uncle Eddie rested. Adelaide bought a fairly prominent marble inlaid headstone and had it placed as customary. She seemed duly proud of the memorial.

Remember that my grandmother and Uncle Eddie were never married. Neither had made any preparations for incapacitation or the inevitable demise of the partner. One day, not long after the accident, an ominous cloud appeared in the personage of Uncle Eddie's long absent brother, who secretively retained himself an attorney and asserted his legal rights to all of the decedent's present property and any compensations due from the workplace accident. He also went after any accumulated pension due to consanguine beneficiaries. The inconsiderate petitioner, his brother, even took the house Uncle Eddie had built. And so, having died intestate and without any dependents, all Eddie's wealth accumulated on self deprivation, went to a brother who showed no concern for Uncle Eddie or his lifetime partner.

There are some things that are legally right but morally wrong. Some things are foreseeable; others aren't as clear. If the focus were kept on right thinking and right actions, most of the problems and turpitude we encounter would never be. Shylock, of Shakespeare's The Merchant of Venice, had overwhelming rights under the law. But is a deal in which a man's flesh is on the table a contract one should even think of, much less create and be ready to execute? So, like a far-away carrion crow perched high, awakened, and excited by the whiff of death, the petitioner made haste and with black vulturous wings, he swooped upon the spoils of his brother's passing, gobbling greedily and hurriedly lest another of his kind came to share or human conscience managed to interpose. Adelaide, assisted by my mother and an attorney, reached a lopsided settlement with the plaintiff.

Turned out of the company's house some months later, Adelaide lived with my mother and her partner for a few months and then came her turn to be placed in the Alms House on Brickdam—the dreadful, retributive circle complete and bound tight.

It seems that life is repetitive and coincidences less uncommon than we think. The person who Mommy had lived with unmarried, after her separation from Daddy, one Mr. Edward, collapsed at work and died on the way to hospital. Like her mother's Edward, Mommy's Edward was conveyed past her on his way to the hospital, dead on arrival. They had nothing saved, and Mommy was now confronted with the possibility of her later years being identical to that of her mother and her mother's mother. Destined to walk the same long road, to the same home for the indigent, to climb slowly the same stairs to bed and board, awaiting the grace of the eternal shade.

We, Albert, and Elaine's children determined that disregard for filial duty shall stop with our generation. No more! Not one more! It matters not what poor choices led to their crises. Ours was not a duty to calculate, blame, and apportion accordingly. We chose to remember that we ate when they ate; sometimes we ate because they didn't eat. Our needs were met before theirs. Under the same corrugated metal roof we slept in their protective care. When the journey was long, they lifted and carried us. When we were sick, no medicine was too expensive. They endured fatigue, loss of much-needed sleep without complaint and that stated was the minimum recount of their aid and parental affection. How now is there any difference? How now could we talk of "inconvenience" or "no room to put her"? What could have led our society to believe that, somehow, our duty to our parents, grandparents and other kin is something we can relinquish and disregard? How is it that aged parents uncared for, brings upon kin no charring social opprobrium?

We have to look to our ancestors for instructive inspiration on how we ought to conduct our lives. They teach us orally and demonstrably. Sometimes by observing their mistakes we might be the wiser. "Nothing comes from corn but corn."

CHAPTER IX

OUR VISIT TO HIS FATHER

I REMEMBER VIVIDLY the night Daddy decided to take me to see my grandfather. He said everyone had met his father but me, so he'd take me on the trip. I was very excited about the journey itself, but also about being with my father. I must have been about seven or eight years old. For an adult, especially one who was familiar with the transportation and landscape, undertaking the journey could be daunting. There were few sights to see, since more than 70 percent of the river's banks was forested. For me, the trip was amazing even before we departed.

Mommy and my siblings talked about the city of Georgetown, the train and its stops, the major stations, the rivers and the ferryboat, and the town of New Amsterdam. My imagination was unrestrained. I was excited and ready for all of it.

Daddy and I set out about 5:30 p.m. on a Friday. He had worked a normal day and had had just an hour between his "knock-off" time and our departure—the launch of the first leg of what to him would have been a grueling journey ahead. He was going to visit his father. We embarked the Betty J, a broad, deep, wooden vessel painted cream with some green on the frames of the windows and trims, bow to stern. About fifty passengers were aboard, mostly men going to see their families and a few business women going to make purchases for their small stores or stalls or maybe returning home having sold their goods. Many of the younger men traveled on the roof of the vessel. There they chatted, drank a bit, or just reposed.

Daddy and I sat in silence on hard benches that ran the length of the boat's sides. We happened to be seated near the engine, a small diesel that needed to be cranked vigorously to get working but, once fired up, produced a cloud of thick blue-gray smoke that swirled and enveloped us. The billows occasioned teariness, along with paroxysms of coughing and choking among some of the passengers seated on benches with backrests positioned across the width and toward the middle of the boat.

As the motor picked up, it smoked less, and the wind passing through the vessel blew away to the rear whatever small amount was still generated. Then it was clear again. I soon got accustomed to my surroundings and relaxed. I looked out the window at the mangroves' gigantic roots, which captured my interest until darkness fell, blanketing everything but the dim interior of the boat. Most of the passengers sat patiently and seldom spoke. Some dozed, probably lulled by the monotonous chug, chug of the boat's engine.

Two dollars, sixty-five miles, eight hours, and sore buttocks later, we disembarked at Stabroek Market wharf in Georgetown. We had about seven hours to wait before setting off to join the 8:00 a.m. train for Rosignol, a small plantation town sixty miles away at the mouth of Berbice River. Some of the passengers set out for various parts of the city. Daddy and I spent the rest of the night at the wharf, as did a few other passengers. Daddy said it made no sense going to a hotel just for a few hours. I didn't mind. He was right. We sat on some crates, Daddy, his head bowed in light sleep. He must have been so tired, I thought.

I sat for a long time listening and observing. I was curious about the hucksters and the small boats unloading plantains, cassava, coconuts, mangoes, and various other produce; there were lots of leafy greens and varieties of fish and shrimp. These people were hard at work, readying for Saturday morning's shoppers, for the best day for sales. This was a side of life I had never seen on this scale before. Women and men were busy at work. Sometimes adolescents worked shoulder-to-shoulder with their parents. Young and old were there in the hubbub—the entire family's shoulder to the wheel. Among a few of the families were very young children, some barely toddlers asleep in their mother's arms or on cardboard on the wharf's floor. I knew it had to be hard on these determined folk—the invisible class, who slog on, through sun or blessed rain, to sustain cities but never get rich, no matter how hard or how long they labor. And they know that.

    I laid myself on a large crate. It must have been the rhythmic lapping of swells against the piles beneath the gentle wind accompanying the incoming tide that lulled me to sleep, mostly undisturbed, by the resonant ding-dong of Stabroek Market's four-faced striking clock, proclaiming each the number of clangs and every thirty-minute interval a single strike. Daddy sat up all night as far as I could tell. Whenever I briefly awoke, he was sitting beside me, head bowed, catching a wink.

Dawn's incipience was easy to miss at first, but not for long; she was slow to visit, but when she did, ah! Just being alive to see it gave its own gratification. She came in a weak gray; morphed crimson; and then poured in shades of blue-pink, orange, and yellow. And then a radiant burst of golden sunshine, companioned by sparse clouds and wafting, salty breeze. It was so beautiful and refreshing. The bustle's pace on the wharf increased to what seemed to me a frenzy—packing, fetching, fixing, talking; laughter here, yelling there; all performing for Saturday's vital commerce. Daddy and I walked through the market, out the red, wrought iron gates where the municipal constable stood guard and into the famous Water Street and the smell of the city. We walked among yellow municipal busses, taxicabs, dray carts, bicycles, pushcarts, and pedestrians—all on well-known missions, certain of their whereabouts and their destinations.

A great pleasure it was, seeing flowering shrubbery, hibiscus, and bougainvillea, all displayed and honoring the dawn.

The city had paved roads and concrete sidewalks. It seemed easy to navigate, since all the streets ran either east to west or north to south. Daddy pointed out landmarks I should know, occasionally telling some history associated with them. I admired the city's well-cared shrubbery and clipped parapets, its lawns, and decorative trees. There were so many shades of green evident, competing with the bright colors of flowers. Some pedestrian pathways were lined with leafy oaks forming shady, domed canopies, all overseen by palm trees standing sentinel at fixed intervals on each side. But the crown of the morning belonged to the many Flamboyant trees blooming red and some pink. I loved every moment.

I liked the clipitty-clop of the horses going by—trotting briskly if pulling an empty cart, depositing dung and urine on the run, their contribution to the city's earthy pungency—and the watchful, formidable, mounted policemen in black uniforms with their distinctive, red-stripped black trousers, the same as their hats. Stout, partially sheathed, long batons hung from polished saddles that creaked as the rider's weight shifted. Traffic policemen were on duty at busy intersections. Peculiar were their white-topped hats and long white sleeves, starched and well ironed. Their confident directing and drilled turns were a performance in itself. Cecil was to become a policeman some years later, and just guess who followed him.

Daddy loved to walk. It was easy for him with his long legs and steady strides. He was patient with me trying to keep up. On the way, we stopped at a busy Chinese restaurant in a poor area somewhere in or near Tiger Bay. He bought me breakfast. He never liked eating out. He said some bananas would be sufficient for him, but I, he said, needed breakfast. He bought me pepper pot, bread, and hot tea. I ate quickly, hungrily I should say. Since lunch yesterday, we'd had nothing. Finished, we then set out for the train station on Carmichael Street. We didn't talk much, but he did continue to point out important places. It was a long walk, but since I had no idea where the trek would end, the morning was so cool, and the city so new and beautiful, I just kept going—excited just to be there.

We arrived at Georgetown Railway Station about thirty minutes early. The rail yard was situated at the lively juncture of Carmichael and Lamaha Streets. The wooden, one-flat station was painted white, trimmed gray, and boasted many large glass- paned windows. One entered the welcoming interior by way of two tall, expansive doorways very close to the street. A cavernous ceiling bearing slow hanging fans created a cool, natural airiness to the cream-colored interior. Polished wooden benches and a ticket counter nicely enhanced the decor of the spick-and-span, wooden-floored public area. Surely, the antiquated chiming clock must be weary of its brass being buffed bright so shiny it was. Though people were milling in and about the terminal, it really was not a busy place, if one were on familiar ground, that is. Up three wide steps, now treaded smooth by generations of passengers and diligently scrubbed and scented, we arrived at the boarding platform.

The steam-powered locomotive, enormous and noisy, idled a little way up the tracks. Its grandeur snatched and jealously held one's attention. So different was it from the newer, quieter diesel types used to move ore cars at the bauxite mines around McKenzie. I was awestruck, this being the first time I had ever seen the likes of such a machine. It was black and shiny, but for gold lettering and other signage. And, oh, the mechanics of the thing! Huge wheels turned by steam-driven pistons. Fire roared, and thick clouds of smoke were released by steam pressure, like a giant's weary sighs. The clang of a polished brass bell mounted atop the boiler chamber at the forward portion of the locomotive, a signal from the officious stationmaster, and we were on the ready.

Per the terminal platform's big clock's Roman numerals, we rolled on the dot of eight as scheduled. The engineer acknowledged the stationmaster's pocket whistle and wave. With great belches of steam and smoke and the reverberant judgment-day Klaxon, the locomotive heaved, carriages swayed, and passengers rocked as the mighty wheels churned their way toward our destination. Who knew that, some years later, I would be riding these same trains on duty as a police constable protecting mail and payroll.

We traveled second-class. Daddy allowed me to walk around. The hucksters were mainly the third-class passengers, burdened by boxes, baskets, stools, jute bags, and other indispensables of their trade. I did get a peek at the spick-and-span, polished brass, first-class compartment with its pretentious, black leather upholstered seats, all so overstuffed, all empty. Not a soul warmed the first-class carriage hauled back and forth every day on the off chance that some well-to-do person or aspirant wanted to travel.

Daddy and I sat together rocking side to side, back and forth on wood-slatted benches in rhythmic lurching and jerks now and then, as we rolled our way to Rosignol. He gave me the window seat, and I spent hours awed by the bucolic scenery, fast appearing, and too soon gone. There were lots of stops, some unremarkable. Mailbags were exchanged and sundry cargo, but the major stations were spectacles worth the wait.

Buxton was the first of the notable stops. Maybe that was because it was a good snack time, but I lend more importance to the sights. Tall, African women, arms no strangers to toil, wearing colorful head wraps worked in concert in a festival of commerce. These women's lives were commingled with the arrival and departures of the trains. On their heads, they bore wooden trays or weaved baskets crammed with ripe fruits. Among these were mangoes of diverse kinds, but none surpassing the prized Buxton Spice. There too were bananas of long, short, or stubby varieties; brown sapodilla; purple star apples and custard apples; quinces; plums; and tangerines—a cornucopia of Buxton's best. Then came their famed crusty, spicy "fish an' bread." If one was in want of cold drink, available were sorrel, mauby, pine drink, and others.

Though simply described, there was a unique culture about the Buxton stop, which passengers looked forward to. These were businesswomen and farmers, who appealed by grabbing your attention for just a second. A smile would lead to the approach, and then, with the sale made and your change given, they would swing immediately to the next potential customer with a smiling inquiry. They had about thirty minutes to compete, make a profit, and be ready for other trains in either direction later in the day. Their children depended on the train and the trade. Others relied on the trains' rumble or the Klaxon's blast to mark the time of day or for starting particular domestic work—it was time to leave the farm or to start cooking. It wouldn't be strange to hear, "Girl, mornin' train done pass. I got to hurry." So entwined was the trains' traffic in the cultural lives of the more provincial villages of British Guiana's coastal region that the two could not be separated. We stopped at the villages Mahaica, and Mahaicony, both of which had large, brown rivers and admirable trestlework bridges. More food vendors, more languorous villages came and went. On and on we rolled, soporific passengers slowly rocked like babies, most already asleep; those awake wished that they too could snooze the ride away—anything to break the monotony, if this wasn't your first trip.

We came upon Abary River, its water black, supposedly deep, both banks thick with hardy, dark green, wild vegetation. Having crossed the Abary, we were now in the County of Berbice, rocking and huff-puffing as lush rice paddy fields now swept past faster, their slender, green stalks rippling their farewell. Yes, this was Berbice, the ancient county, British Guiana's rice basket.

It was now coming on noon, and Daddy sat silently, bearing his characteristic pensive patience. Not I though—my attention was riveted by the windows. I was fascinated by herds of cattle in pastures and fallowed rice paddy fields; villages with historic names, some of Dutch origin, like Weldaad (in English, benefaction, boon, mercy); and the English Fort Wellington. Fellow passengers' restlessness foretold our destination's approach. We rolled into Rosignol Station with three blasts of the horn and disembarked with ease. There was no rush, since we had to wait on the ferryboat to take us across the sprawling, yellow-brown estuary of Berbice River. Daddy stretched with relief but showed no sign of tiredness. We walked idly about the wharf some. Daddy pointed out the delta island, Crab Island. It was fairly large; unpopulated; and thickly covered with wild, dark green, hardy, salt-tolerant vegetation.

Daddy took good care of me throughout the trip and was especially careful with me as we boarded the ferry. I don't recall much of the crossing except that the river was very, very wide. No detail could be discerned as to the eastern bank, but the shimmer of New Amsterdam was unmistakable. We sat on the open upper deck enjoying the sunny afternoon. The wind, a mite stronger than a breeze, cropped the waves' tops, making for a yellow- brown, white-capped, animated seascape. Daddy was enjoying that, I assumed by the smile he countenanced. The wind was full in his clean-shaven face, and his eyes blinked in response. He inhaled deeply of the cool, fresh air. It was indeed a wonderful day. The high, double-decker vessel heaved and canted a bit but caused no disquiet among the passengers. Pulling alongside and securing to the wharf was easy for the well-practiced crew.

Soon we disembarked, this time sprightlier, since most people were rushing, bundles, baskets, and boxes a-hip, to waiting cars for hire. We had no trouble acquiring and sharing one, and then commenced the last portion of our journey.

The long night and day ended about 3:00 p.m. at No. 2 Village, East Canje, Berbice—the residence of my father's father. Daddy made this twenty-one hour, 140-mile sojourn just to be with his father for the weekend and to introduce me to my grandfather. I knew that Daddy was happy because he called me Brods all the time. I loved that and loved him.

My mother always spoke well of my grandfather. Undoubtedly, she respected him very much and liked that he was always excited to see our family. Daddy and I exited the car, and there he was, sitting on the small veranda at the top of his front stairs. I could only concur with her description of him. He shouted excitedly to his wife of many years, Louisa, announcing our arrival—just as Mommy said he would. "Louisa, they're here, they're here!"

Daddy and I ascended the front stairs of the unpainted, wooden house. It stood high on stilts, very common in British Guiana's flood prone coastal plain. The modest house might be best described as worn, rather than old. It was constructed from hardwood abundant in the colony's forests. I could not tell the wood's name, but an informed eye would guess it to be made of greenheart or bullet wood, both well known to outlast generations, so impervious to the elements of tropical climes were they. The steps were now smooth from the many feet and shoes they served and from Louisa's vigorous scouring.

Grandfather fumbled, rising to greet us. "Albert, Albert," he welcomed, opening his big arms to hug, and did so with much effort.

Daddy insisted that he remained seated, kissed his cheek, and introduced me.

We shook hands as I said, "Good afternoon, Grandfather." He looked at me and said, "Hello", with a broad smile.

Grandfather was fussing excitedly; Louisa arrived from within with effusive hugs and kisses for all. Her devotion to my grandfather and my father was quite unmistakable. The aged couple radiantly expressed genuine hospitality and joy. They, in their later years, were getting by economically without complaint or resentment, their needs met by their land's fruits—coconuts, Chinese bitter melons, long beans, eggplant, and whatnot thriving in the backyard. With meager pensions and what monetary help Daddy sent, they were not suffering. Grandfather still cobbled, but rarely. I suspect that was more a hobby, more stubbornness than need. But it offered him something to occupy himself; despite his failing sight and strength and his left knee damaged by the years of using it like an anvil on which to form and tap leather, he continued this practice.

They chatted, lively and beaming, while I marveled. Life was so different here, contrasted to industrial Mackenzie, where light was a switch across the room and water the mere turn of the spigot's head in the kitchen or bathroom, always available, day or night—the subsidized utilities taken for granted.

As the evening progressed, kerosene lamps were lit as the outdoors quickly shaded from gray to the blackest black known. Bedtime came early in the far countryside. We were shown to our room, in fact their room, with the best bed in the house. It was a huge, sturdy bed with sheets so white and starched they shone. I never had the pleasure of seeing such again in my life; these bedcovers had the freshness of soap and being sun dried. An immense mosquito net hung high from the sealing. It engulfed the bed all the way down to the floor. Right there, I learned magnanimity of the heart. Given their means and where they lived, toilsome work and sacrifice were absolutely necessary, primarily by Louisa, just to give us the comfort of two nights in their home. Detour with me for a minute, and let's fully appreciate what she had to have done to make just the bedding I so appreciated that the memory fondly survives. This was, for me, an unspoken lesson in humility. Rural British Guiana was not a place where you did not plan well ahead. There you could not afford to waste a cup of potable water. Frugality and recycling was at a degree where regular garbage collection was really unnecessary. Everything was used and reused until it could no longer serve any purpose. For instance, if one were purchasing cooking oil, one would be expected to provide one's own bottle, into which the commodity was decanted; a jam jar became a receptacle for condensed milk or salt or spices. A can may become a cup, sometimes with a handle attached, and so on. If the can were large enough, a wire lifting handle might be attached, and it then became a usable kitchen utensil. About once a month, maybe less frequently, trash was burned in the open area at the backland. The same went for cooked food; leftover rice might be incorporated into a bake batter (pancake-like batter) for the following day's breakfast.

To afford us the fresh sheet she so impressed us with, Louisa would have had to plan the day to wash. Cloudy today? No? Okay, then get out the scrub board and washtub and set it in the usual place so as to minimize bending. She would have had to go to a public pipe on the street or use collected water from their reservoir—a large, wooden vat or two forty-five gallon drums, most likely the former—and fetch about three buckets of water. Then she would soak the sheets and pillow cases, scrub them while sparingly using a cake of hard soap, rinse and wring the coarse cotton, repurposed from flour sacks, bleached white, and then stitched together. Meanwhile, the hot water would have been ready on the coal pot she had lit and fanned earlier, the coals by then bright red and orange. She'd have used that steaming water to liquefy the pebbles of starch; poured the thick mix into fresh water, to which a cake of "Blue" had been dissolved to enhance whiteness; wrung the sheets; spread them in the sun on a clothesline; and kept an eye on the weather, listening for rain. Once the sheets were crispy dry, Louisa would have had to set a fire to get charcoal burning. She'd have placed the smoldering coals in a cast-iron pressing device, heating that as she concurrently sprinkled the crinkled sheets. Lastly, she would press the bedding, steaming, folding, and pressing the cotton to a fine finish. Such was the work it took just for the bedding—the bedding for her guests. When the weak, softer classes speak philosophically of self-reliance, I doubt they have a blinking clue.

Despite the distant years, I am most grateful to have experienced such selflessness and kindness. I wish I could express to Grandfather and Louisa my gratitude again and again and reciprocate the boundless hospitality they had shown.

Grandfather's son had come to visit.

We rose early the following day. That Sunday was memorable for the tender love shown by my father. It was also the time I saw him most relaxed, which led me to conclude that, when he was irascible, it might have been due to stress rather that chronic annoyance. But that's just speculative; we'll never know the fact. Daddy wore a clean, white, long-sleeved shirt and trousers that were a bit dark, with socks and black shoes. We went first to Rose Hall market—a vivacious, strident place, especially on weekends. It was astounding. A small market even by local standards, Rose Hall was nonetheless sprawling due to vendors squatting peripherally. It offered variety and abundance galore, so pleasing to see. From the lowly, ubiquitous, coconut-derived chip sugar cake to grated sugar cakes, praline pink, and white-layered coconut candy to motley coconut rolls, buns, and cakes to cane juice, mauby, tamarind and sorrel drinks, sweets were abundant. Some vendors displayed their merchandise on bags or mats in the shade of large trees. I saw mounds of jamoon (single-seeded fruit the color of blueberries), watermelon slices, golden apples, tamarind, boiled breadnut, and channa (chickpeas). Sellers offered natural varieties of corn, shelled or on the cob. This was the center of the lower Corentyne region of Berbice and patronized by residents from miles around. Vendors sold fish, haberdashery, household utensils, and heaven knows what else.

Daddy was on very familiar grounds, and it showed. He seemed relaxed, and his unusual chattiness and good humor evidenced he was enjoying this outing. I absolutely loved it. "Brods, look at this," or, "Come, come, Brods. You see this?" he would say as he discovered once more something interesting or familiar to him, but not known to me. Daddy related stories about so many things—so much history he'd witnessed. For him, this was home. And in a manner of speaking, he had come home again. For me, we did not need to converse. Just having my father there, not melancholic, not brooding, was all I needed to be happy.

Daddy was excited and determined to show me Rose Hall Sugar Estate. We trekked toward the tall, smoking chimneys in the distance. A sunny Sunday it was, bright, with mild temperature and no threat of rain clouds. Cool Atlantic trade winds were always a moderating factor. Flat, open land flanked both sides of the bricky, red loam, traffic-free road we walked. One could see miles and miles of verdant fields, some with young sugar cane, other sections cleared and brown, the crop lately harvested leaving for us an earthy smell, pleasant to those who tilled the soil. On a few fallowed fields, young grasses had sprung. Here and there, a tree shaded small herds of cattle, resting unbothered, sleepily chewing the afternoon's monotony away. Some grazed as contented bovines do. Intermittently, a vain, frolicsome calf would tear off, running post-haste, frightened by nothing, chased by nothing, pursuing nothing. The herd, unimpressed by its prancing about, would chew on sedately without interruption. One imagines their weary sigh. "We've seen this before."

There were two parallel trenches on the sides of the road, their purpose to regulate drainage and irrigation of the cane fields. They seemed stagnant at the time, but a closer, careful look gave away their slow flow in a particular direction. The trenches, deep and wide, and the opaque water interested me. Light winds blew shimmering ripples momentarily in different places. But there were concentric ripples also where a bee, a dragonfly, or a wasp dared hover and sip, mostly with success. Occasionally, one heard a quick splash as a houri, a hassa (armored catfish), or other predator lunched on the incautious, or themselves became lunch. The trenches hosted a variety of life, especially since the amphibious found habitat among the cane. A big splash might indicate fish at play or a bird's dunk, but one cannot be sure; the splash might have been an alligator or snake having been lucky. But on we went, a pause here and there to satisfy an interest or pelt a few pebbles into the trenches. An idyllic, enjoyable Sunday it was.

CHAPTER X

A VISIT TO ROSE HALL ESTATE

WE WALKED ABOUT the periphery of the factory. Daddy, having worked a short time in his youth at the estate, knew quite a lot of sugar's cultivation, harvesting, and manufacturing processes. He showed me black-water punt trenches, where big, deep metal barges floated, linked together by heavy chains with enormous links. Some of the barges were filled with harvested sugarcane. A few mules stood on the banks of a trench, the only hint of life among them a sleepy blink or an occasional quick switch of a long tail swatting bothersome insects. The mules were the largest animals I had ever seen. They were very tall—certainly more hands than a big horse—docile, colossal animals. They would sometimes rest a shod leg. With sporadic twitching of ears and quivering the skin they would now and then rid themselves of pesky mosquitoes and flies while waiting imperturbably their next call to haul.

A little further on Daddy showed me steep piles of bagasse and explained further processes in the conversion of the crop to sugar. He didn't stop there. He wanted to show me the whole manufacturing process, step by step, to the finished product. But to do that, we had to get into the factory. We began scouting for entrances and found an open gate toward the back of the building. The only problem, though, was a watchman seated in a nearby hut, and that's where we had to pass. We crossed a dirt patch and stood against the wall of his watch house, and from there, we watched the watchman, fully engrossed in his lunch. Daddy waited, timing his motions. Our other advantage, besides the watchmen meal, was the noise of the factory's engines.

There was about twenty feet of vulnerability for us. Daddy told me to wait, and he crossed first. He did not appear stealthy. In fact, he walked quietly, confidently on the watchman's blind side. The watchman just kept gorging, unaware of anything beyond his bowl. Daddy beckoned me to follow as prearranged, and I accomplished the task as he had. Then, father and son, we walked jauntily into the factory, interlopers we.

Daddy took me to the second floor and showed me huge gears and revolving choppers with razor-sharp blades, shiny and efficient, mincing tons of cane stalk fed them night and day. Off we went to the grinders—gigantic ribbed rotors crushing, squeezing the last drop that could possibly be scrunched from the cane. I was amazed. We walked over to the towering treatment vats, where he showed me valves, thermostats, pressure gauges, volumeters, and other miscellaneous gadgetry. He certainly knew the workings of the factory and explained them well.

At the molasses tank, we were approached by a worker. An Indian man of average height. I guessed he was in his early thirties, nothing distinguishing about his dress. Apparently, he thought Daddy was a manager or inspector—surely someone with authority. He greeted us formally and, without asking who we were, related a litany of grievances. Daddy tilted his head affecting grave interest, nodded his empathy, spoke little but promised to "look into" the complaints. As we pressed on, another couple of workers made the same error, and Daddy responded as before. He was careful to do nothing to discourage his advantage of their misperception. In fact, he walked casually, his hands clasped behind his back, his bearing inspectorial. The group of workers had grown to about eight, each eager to tell of his suffering as Daddy feigned interest. Well, now we had free rein of the factory floors. Daddy was exuberant. "Taste this, Brods. This is the purified cane juice," he shouted above the industrial din of the sugar factory.

Without being asked, a worker readily produced his battered tin cup, from which I tasted the clear, intensely sweet, hot liquid drawn from one of the open concrete pools.

Daddy and I were having a great time on this adventurous trespass, and I was encouraged to sample each stage, from cane juice to sugar crystals, light and dark. We went downstairs to a cavernous concrete storage bond containing mounds of sugar. The crystals were piled the height of a dozen men. Yes, at the foot of the sugar hills I was as close as one can be represented to be as a kid in a candy shop. Finally, we said good-bye to the good-natured staff and walked calmly toward the exit of the premises. But there was that watchman again. And this time, having already sated himself, he seemed alert.

The watchman was positioned between us and the gate. He stood with an air of boldness, curiously observing us, but yet unsure of what to do. So, he waited and watched as a watchman would. We walked confidently in his direction, stopping briefly to look at fish in a pond, some ornamental vegetation or some such insignificant thing. We made a show of idleness, as directed by my father, and then sauntered amiably up to the watchman, creating visible consternation in the poor man.

Daddy, quite relaxed, paused to speak with the befuddled watchman, who, if nothing else, certainly understood his own dilemma. That is to say, the fellow would be reasoning thus: If this stranger, had no right to be in there, how could he explain not having challenged the stranger on the way in? Should the man turn out to be a manager, an inspector, or worse…. Oh, God, help me! If the stranger was some even higher official, as he appeared to be, evidenced by his light complexion, dress and bearing, his (the watchman's) goose was cooked. He would have been expected to know the official. Oh, God, it's Sunday! How could I have missed him?

But the watchman was cleverer than we'd presumed. On our approach to the gate near by the guardhouse, our watchman beaming and confident in his khaki shirt and shorts, pretended to be quite aware of our entry and hoped that everything was to Daddy's satisfaction. He kept talking. His loquacity was either the result of nervous anxiety or a cunning maneuver to disallow Daddy the space to ask him questions. He spoke agreeably with Daddy, occasionally darting a swift appraising look at me. Well, if he is touring with his little boy, this white-shirted man must be "somebody important," he seemed to be thinking. The watchman was careful to ask no questions, while dearly hoping to be asked none. He expressed that it was a fine day and, "No, no, there hasn't been any problem at all; all day, nothing," he said blithely, with unmistakable self-satisfaction, but earnest in his desire to see the last of us. Daddy nodded a great show of approval, much pleasuring the watchman.

We wished him a good evening and casually walked off the estate. All was well, but looking back I noticed the watchman had not returned to his repose in the guardhouse. Instead, he vigilantly paced the vicinity. We laughed a good laugh. I was happy to be with my father; he was in such buoyant spirits, and I loved him.

Well, all things must end—sometimes, regrettably, not as we might have wished. We began our journey home to Grandfather's. Now the trek seemed so much longer; what had just recently been noticed and stirred wonder was now just a long, dirt road I wished to see the end of, the sooner the better. The various shades of green vegetation once adored and the cattle in spacious pastures now became, in my eyes, nothing but bush, grass and unremarkable animals. My heavy leather shoes, worn without socks, were rasping my heels, and my right pinky toe was bruised.

I did not care whether the houri caught the dragonfly, an alligator caught the houri, or the butterfly caught a toad. Let's be home!

But this was where we were to pay for the day's pleasures and tomfoolery. It hadn't occurred to either of us that I had been ingesting way too much sugary substances, which may have caused temporary hyperglycemia. At first, I started feeling not just right. Then a dizzying nausea got a grip of me. Dazed, I tried to keep up but was stumbling and lagging. Daddy noticed that something was wrong and asked if I was okay. I told him I had "bad feelings" (nausea in the colloquialism of the time in British Guiana). He just patiently assessed the situation. "Well," he said amiably, "We don't have much farther to go."

He lifted me and sat me on his shoulders. I held him around his neck as he strode unfalteringly all the way home. It had to be very tiring for him because, when we got to Grandfather's, he stood beside the stairs, allowing me an easy dismount and saving himself from having to bend over. He gave a long, even sigh. Home at last. This shared experience was among the best memories of my father, and I will always fondly remember that episode of our lives.

CHAPTER XI

MAKING LEMONADE

MY SISTER, DOLLY, toughed it out. She was a fighter. As I mentioned earlier, Dolly always picked fights with me. I still have a two-inch scar on my upper right arm from a razor blade she cut me with. On my right thigh, I have a scar from her bite. Both became infected. Nothing from my parents.

All of her belligerence stopped one Saturday morning when, frustrated at some other matter, she came charging headfirst, met my right fist with her nose, and gave up some blood. She screamed. Our neighbor rushed over and diffused our differences. Never again did we fight or even get into heated arguments.

All the attention showered on her in preadolescence, I think, was insufficient to spare her (what I now believe to be) neglect of her emotional needs at what was another critical stage of her development. Looking back, I suspect she might have had poor self-esteem. Dolly sucked two of her right fingers into mid-childhood, possibly a self-soothing behavior or indicative of anxiety. She struggled with nocturnal bedwetting, clinically called enuresis. She was so ashamed, especially since she had to put the bedding outdoors to dry, thus proclaiming her difficulties to all the neighbors. Every time it occurred, Mommy was upset with her and might have said some things that were counterproductive to Dolly's ego development. Her disorder was left untreated and unmanaged. When she was about twelve years old, the bedwetting just ceased, suggesting that, like Dennis's symptoms, the etiology was probably not organic in nature.

Dolly attended school regularly, always clean and bright in her navy-blue skirt, yellow cotton shirt, ribbons, socks, and shoes. Dolly did the best she could with the hand she was dealt. By then the Ministry of Education, situated in Georgetown, seemed to regard chaos as an acceptable management stratagem. Students sometimes had no idea what examinations they were being prepared for, and the books changed arbitrarily. Often new mandates came amid competing curriculum and with no understanding of local situations, for example, the exponential population growth in the MacKenzie area. At one time there were thirty-eight students in my class, and the same was true in Dolly's I suppose. The school had become a place that reinforced low expectations and dismal outcomes.

As a kid, Dolly's fantasy of highest gratification was that she would get a brand-new bicycle and a "tight skirt," fashionable at the time, and, according to her, "ride to work at the office every day." It was not that she was incapable. She just did not have the guidance and inspiration to help her focus on learning. Worse still, after Mommy left, she assumed most of the money management and cooking, constantly worrying about what to cook today. Dolly attended a typing and office practice course and, not surprisingly, she married early.

What is remarkable about my sisters, especially Dolly, is that, from a young age, they understood their duty to work. Fanciful as the thought of a tight skirt was and opportunities for her as a female, narrow at best, she persevered. But she was fine. Daddy never shirked his obligations, and thus we never suffered.

Dolly married Teekahram Persaud, then a police constable stationed at MacKenzie. Theirs turned out to be a strong, lasting union, despite the pressures of it being an interracial marriage. Romeo and Juliet's parents' mistake was yielding to community pressures. Daddy was 100 percent supportive of Dolly and Teekahram, despite rude, dissuasive remarks from some in the town. Daddy was very impressed with Teeka, and Dolly's husband, in turn, respected Daddy. I know of no time that there was ever a harsh word between them. So close were they that Daddy, later in life, would ask that Teeka handle his funeral rites and cremation. But I'm getting a little ahead of myself.

Mommy was approving of the union too, and so was our whole family. But Dolly had the gifts of fortitude, modest needs, and steadfast friendships. People easily gravitated to dimpled Dolly. Her home was near our family home, and Daddy routinely stopped for an hour or two to chat with the family and play with his grandchildren.

Impediments notwithstanding, Teeka and Dolly were, in relatively short time, able to save enough money and migrated to the United States. Living in New York City, they worked spiritedly, improved their possibilities, and soon brought their children. They all became United States citizens and continued their excellence. Later, they invited Daddy to New York on a long visit. He stayed with them close to two years and thoroughly enjoyed the city, often remarking that he never thought he would have had such a great opportunity as to visit New York. The socioeconomic opposition he struggled against, given his situation of birth, along with physical disablement, must have demanded steely grit of no small measure, in itself an admirable accomplishment.

Asked to recount an affectionate memory of our father, Dolly related that she and Dennis lived with our grandmother, Adelaide, for some months, and Daddy would visit them often between his lunch breaks. Once, when both children were sick, he got upset with Adelaide over their care; he went to the pharmacy, where he bought them medicine. Later, he returned with soup he had himself cooked for them. Her abiding memories of his life are his exceptional generosity and his steadfastness as a dependable provider.

Maternal bonding between my mother and Pinkey, alluded to earlier, lasted to such a dysfunctional degree that it must have affected both of them negatively all through their lives. Try to imagine a five-year-old with attachment disorder so severe that it ultimately stymied her emotional development, I believe. Mommy never left Pinkey. It got so bad that my mother had the task of her life introducing any normal separation between them, at times literally dragging Pinkey to school, prying her little hands finger by finger from whatever she'd grabbed onto, be it a doorpost, a banister, a garbage bin, a concrete culvert, the school's chain-link perimeter fence, or anything else her small hands could reach. Pinkey would wail all the way, and she resisted mightily for such a little one, so determined was she not to be parted from Mommy. It was a spectacular test of wills, each step forward a small victory for Mommy. My mother would be short of breath after getting her into class, but then Pinkey would run out of the class back to my mother, renewing the contest once more. Nobody but Pinkey could have that amount of tears.

It took quite a while to get her stable in school. But once settled, she made the best of her opportunities.

Pinkey seemed quite happy to play all by herself in the afternoons. Her specialty was play school. Her imagined students sat in three rows on the steps at the back of the house. There were about nine kids in her fantasy class, sometimes more depending on her mood at the moment, but the daily script was the same. Before class began, she would get a stick, whip, belt, or any implement suitable for the afternoon's circumstances. Standing at the school's doorway, she would don a look and tone so stern one could only imagine the trepidation of the little arrivals. Dickens could not have devised and described, without much distress to himself, Pinkey's fictional school.

"You, mister." She would accost the young pupil whom she deemed tardy. "Why are you late for class?"

"Oh, the rain?" she would taunt rhetorically. "The rain did not stop me from being here on time. Eight o'clock is eight o'clock!"

Whack, flail, licks!

"Oh, yo' still cryin'? I'll give you something to cry for."

Smack, whip, more licks, and protracted scolding, often all delivered concurrently, would ensue.

Pinkey's penchant for dominance and control was noticeable to even a casual observer. Having spanked all who arrived late, and there was always a sufficient number who were unpunctual, Pinkey would move on to disciplining those who sat in the wrong seat, those deemed inattentive or distracted, and any who were talking. In fact, if her students breathed too deeply, corporal punishment might visit them without delay. She taught only arithmetic and spelling, but her style was, without deviation, interrogative and deprecatory.

Pinkey would pace back and forth, hands clasped behind her back, whip firmly grasped, affecting an air of final authority as she asked questions of the stairs. Predictably, her pupils gave the wrong answers, and the beatings began all over again. When the whip was shredded and useless, she got another, and yet another still. Sometimes, the sole of a shoe would suit her purpose. There were no bright students in her make-believe school. Her obsession with order and discipline was something to study. She breathlessly spanked those imagined kids with amazing vigor. She spared or praised none. Thank God for sunset, our curfew time, when her school was dismissed with an ultimate threat about the homework due tomorrow.

Her play was amusing to me at the time, but so much can be learned about families if one observes studiously their children at play. Thank God, Pinkey never became a teacher or corrections officer. That would have been disastrous for the population under her supervision. I shudder! But is anyone in doubt as to where she learned the behaviors—whose actions she mimicked to the T, so to speak? How, in her young, pliable mind did she conclude that any error, no matter how trivial, must never be overlooked— that it was unerringly traceable to lack of order, respect and obedience and that punishment must, of necessity, be physical, swift, strong, and unrelenting as it intensified? How did she arrive at this mind-set that construed discipline as synonymous with violence?

Children learn best by what they see. They also imitate what they witness and readily employ long-imprinted attitudes, sometimes with very unfortunate consequences. This child was exhibiting deeply ingrained plantation ethics, which lean predominantly toward judgmental attitudes and strong emphasis on unhesitating obedience. As the youngest child, where best might her values find expression than the absolute control of fictive classrooms of young, powerless children?

But Pinkey had simple plans for her future. She expressed oftentimes that, when she grew up, she would work; when paid, she would buy her own peanut butter, lots and lots of peanut butter, and fill her kitchen cabinet with it. So glad I am that she is now able to afford her needs and that there is such variety in peanut butter. I do hope she is never out of the complementary freshly baked bread.

Soon after Daddy's return from New York, he moved to Georgetown, where he lived comfortably with Pinkey. Not accustomed to idleness, he rose early and went walking, usually to the sea wall. He always loved the open air. He did the produce shopping at Kitty Market mostly. When in the mood, he was known to go all the way to Bourda Market or even Stabroek once fired up. Though taxis and buses were available and affordable to him, he would walk for miles, only because he enjoyed it. He did as much as possible to get things ready before Pinkey's arrival from work, sparing her some of the extra steps necessary to complete preparing dinner. Those in the community who knew him commented on how clean Pinkey kept her father. He changed his diet to predominantly vegan, seeming to find that beneficial for his body.

Pinkey reports that Daddy was good company for her and, she listened when he wanted to talk reminiscently. On one of her birthdays, he walked all the way downtown and back just to buy her a gift. It was a beautiful gold brooch, now a cherished memento.

CHAPTER XII

DUTY BOUND

> There is one duty so Universal and obvious that it is seldom mentioned: the mother's duty to raise her children, provided that they are suffered to live. Another duty - equally primitive, I believe, in the human race - is incumbent on the married man: the protection and support of his family. The parents' duty of taking care of their offspring is, in the first place, based on the sentiment of parental affection.
>
> — Edvard Westermarck
> The Origin and Development of the Moral Ideas
> (Macmillan: London, 1906)

IN THE EARLY years, our family struggled to make ends meet, but my parents were undauntedly industrious and creative. We baked a variety of cakes and sold them with homemade drinks at nearby construction sites. We spent many nights manually truncating coconuts and pineapples for filling small cakes, tarts, and rolls. We grated cassava for pone and made corn pone too, all in a small kitchen dominated by a six-burner cast-iron, wood-burning stove, accompanied by two modest tables, an enameled sink, and a shower room. The sorrel, ginger, pineapple, and mauby drinks had to be spiced and sweetened. Everyone had a chore in the weekday evenings. To this day, I cannot see how that was orchestrated. I respect both of my parents for their faith and grit.

About that time, my father had just found work with a Canadian bauxite mining company. He was later to move up to plumber and then machinist. He was so proud and always counseled us to learn a trade. It would "keep you out of the sun and the rain," he would tell us. On weekends he did some private work setting up cisterns and indoor plumbing for houses across the river. My father worked indefatigably.

Sometimes he would take me along as a little helper. For what work I actually did, the real reason had to have been that he just wanted company. He worked without a break, without even a pause to eat. In fact, he carried no food. He just worked until the goal he'd set himself was met and my vision dark from hunger. He earned well and was very charitable. Such was the dependable provider I knew.

We all called him Daddy; even as adults, we continued. He called me Brods when he was cheerful or relaxed, but some of the time, it was, "Yo, boy," or, "Yo, lazy bitch." For me that translated as, "Caution, slippery surface; use extreme care." But my brothers got the same descriptive criticism.

Daddy didn't call me by my first name much. Our relationship was a complex one. I was tense in his presence and did not know how to react when he was gentle. Too much ambivalence, I guess. We were to become colder, impassively polite, and more formal as I grew through my difficult teens after our mother left. That we will cover subsequently.

There were two categories of work my father was contemptuous of—cane cutting (manual harvesting of sugarcane) and what he called "working in White people's kitchens." This was a reference to the domestic servants of the 100 percent Caucasian, expatriate, managerial staff, who imprisoned themselves under guard of their private constabulary headed by a British major (retired). Management staff resided at Watooka and Richmond Hill, a few miles away, and required domestic servants to free them of housework so that they could pursue their liberties. As to cane cutting, it was backbreaking toil in tropical elements. Cutting cane was dangerous, burdensome work for meager pay and stingy benefits. These were the least desirable of occupations, and Daddy was constantly using them as motivators to get us to take advantage of educational opportunities. An admonishing lecture from my father seemed interminable, but the essence of his advice was beneficial. Some years later, I wrote him a letter thanking him for his exhortations. Pinkey, my sister, related that he was so proud that he carried it around in his pocket for quite sometime, showing it to friends and relatives. I was surprised and gratified, that a thing so simple made him so pleased and proud.

Life is neither equal nor fair. That is so incontrovertible I wish I didn't have to state it. But there's this falsity out there that distorts our perception of reality and misleads us to faulty conclusions. Firmly held beliefs are retained, despite all the evidence of history and the present—evidence that yells at us, calling our attention in an attempt to inform us that life in fact is brutal, random and by no means serene, regardless of where on our globe one happens to be. "Work in White people's kitchens," Daddy called it. Racist?

Not a bit of it, but not thoughtfully presented either.

Another job among the lowest of the low, according to Daddy, was "working for Valcin," a black immigrant from the French- speaking Caribbean, contracted to provide the town's sanitation services. Valcin fulfilled his obligations by means a shade away from indentured servitude and peonage. He hired none of the local people because the higher wages would diminish his profit. To optimize success, he arranged to recruit men from his hometown in the Caribbean. All expenses paid. As they worked he deducted the cost of sponsorship, boarding and lodging. When Valcin rode past on his inspections, one had better be not only actually working, but also well advanced in his assigned task. The working conditions and relationship between employer and "employee" were a spectacle right out of Cool Hand Luke, absent the prison fence. Not once did I see Valcin dismount and have a casual conversation with one of his workers.

Many of us tend to look down our noses at whatever way another chooses to make a living. Doing so is easier and more self- complimentary than the alternative. Still, chooses might actually be the wrong word; a look at social history makes it clear that, for most people, a "career path" means inadvertently tumbling into a job and then finding themselves unable to leave, though free to do so.

I love to hear talk about the "dignity of labor." But there is never enough said in favor of the labor of those who make society function, especially those whose hands get dirty.

I am keenly aware of this imbalance, as I have had opportunities to, sometimes actually and other times vicariously, experience different positions on the continuum. Perhaps that's why Markham's poem, "The Man With the Hoe" and Frederick Douglas' anecdotal "Cast Down Your Bucket Where You Are" appeal to me politically.

We shall see later that, but for the domestic servants' earnings in "White people's kitchens, Mommy's business venture might not have prospered as it did, and I might not have been able to be here writing at leisure.

My counsel is to take immediately, what jobs are available to you, learn marketable skills, and continue to search for better as you keep on improving yourself.

CHAPTER XIII

SHARING THE PAIN

AFTER MY OLDER three siblings left home for work in the city, Georgetown, and England, our family at home consisted of both parents, me, and my two young sisters—yes, the second family. My parents' marriage floundered and wrecked. My father, disappointed, hurt, and ashamed, changed profoundly, for his wife left and he knew she wasn't returning. He began arriving home later from work. Sometimes he would go straight to the movies, something he'd previously never done without first coming home. Other times, he'd idle outside a dance hall, listening to the music of youth and talking with others "passing time." Maybe he did not want to come home anymore. On the occasions of a good mood, he would tell us about his evening. One movie that he liked was Django, a Western shoot-'em-up film of the sixties. We would have good nights sometimes, like when he came home having listened to Wilson Pickett's, "Land of a Thousand Dances." He sang and mimicked the dance moves, and we all laughed.

Some evenings his cronies, about six of them, would come by after work. They included Mr. Massay, Lynch, Zepher, Sugar, and Clarke. Since visits from his friends were unprecedented, it was sound conjecture that it was their way of cheering him up a bit. They'd drink a little rum from shot glasses; laugh; and have lofty, lengthy, tangential discussions. No one was ever disagreeable, loud, or overly inebriated, and they all left at reasonable hours. I respected these men for their compassion and thoughtful support. Daddy surely needed it.

I could not begin to imagine how solitary and abandoned Daddy must have felt. His first three children were gone, their letters and cards irregular and few. None appeared to mark his birthday, Fathers' Day, or even Christmas. Carmen wrote from England a few times. Now his wife was gone too, and to his mind, his children were all gearing up to leave the home. His love lost and labor expended, his duty, love, and charity must all have seemed unreciprocated.

I continued making his daily oatmeal, which he ate silently at the kitchen table near one of two wood-slatted windows. I had begun taking care of that when I was about ten or so. Sometimes, it would be sago, cornmeal, blancmange, or chocolate milk and a hamburger, the latter bought from the nearby market. But he clearly preferred oatmeal, his favorite dish. Daddy left us to ourselves more and more and never planned for anything. The ritual was, on Wednesday nights, he signed his paycheck and left it on the table with his tag. It was my job to go to the Royal Bank of Canada's long line outside the pay window, cash his check, and leave the envelope of cash on the table. He would then give Dolly the "house money." She would prepare food for the week. Kids learn early to take care of themselves and a home. When cash was short, we cooked green papaya in curry with rice. Sometimes we boiled eggs and rice. But most of the time we had fair meals. I was desperately looking for work. I was eighteen and ineligible to continue work at the post office, where I had been employed since months short of my fifteenth birthday. I wondered who could have made such silly policy that benefitted no one. It was probably connected to a colonial relic of apprenticeship that no one got interested in changing.

Somehow, unfortunately, Daddy got it in his mind that I knew about my mother's drift. In fact, I was the last of their children to know. I was told by Dennis one morning as he brushed his teeth, preparing for work. It was just a flat, almost rhetorical question, really.

"Do you know …?" he said.

I replied sharply, "No," with unmistakable finality and busied myself with some trivia to avoid talk.

Surely, Dennis sensed that I did not want to hear another word; that was the end of the conversation, if it could be called that. My blood chilled, and he left for work. However, something else was in process here—my loyalty. Sons are protective of their mothers, and that includes any assail on her character.

So, what we faced was divided loyalties. Much literature is present on the subject. Most religious, secular, philosophical, and ethical guidance give lots to ponder but no clear answers relative to older children in the perplexing quagmire of showing fidelity to two parents when one has not given it to the other. The best I got was a duty to follow that which produces the greatest good; another piece of advice was to serve the highest virtue, regardless of the outcome. Still another counsel advises one to follow the dictates of one's own conscience.

There is a moral duty of all kin to do what is best to maintain the wholeness of the family, to protect its integrity from whatever may cause shame or unhappiness. Noah's sons, Shem and Zaphet, covered their drunken father's nakedness with their coats, protecting him from shame and ridicule (Genesis 9:21–25).

But should a child venture to tell either parent such devastating news? And how does a son broach that subject with his father?

Isn't there the risk of shaming and angering both parents, alienating each of them? How do you approach the topic when all the clues are so flagrant that surely he preferred to be willfully blind?

Can anyone be certain what route to take when the repercussions of a disclosure might well be serious violence, even murder of the spouse or the third person? Can anyone know how the scorned spouse, forced to acknowledge the elephants everyone has been tiptoeing around, act to save face. In times past, the bearer of bad news soon made unwanted acquaintance with his executioner.

Given the chance, if not likelihood, that the family could lose both parents were a secret spoken, there is good reason for percipient silence. And so all these elephants were ceaselessly romping, stomping, and blaring trumpets in the house. But no one was dealing with the cacophony.

Still, everything must end. Planned or unplanned, an end will always come. One night, having grown weary, his heart stuffed full of all his repressed anger and bitterness, my father let loose with churlish vociferation. Long past issues were regurgitated, recounted, and displayed for us, my parents' children, and for our neighbors. Finally came his crudely stated ultimatum. Mommy responded little, lest he become more incensed. But they both knew this final clash had been long in the making and bound to happen, since no reconciliatory efforts had been made.

Dead. Dead! This marriage was dead, with no resuscitative possibilities. It had been painfully ailing for a long time. A few days later, it was put down to eternal rest. The last of the elephants, work done, ambled its way out of the home.

When families collapse, all members pay, some more than others. This collection of the debt might even reach beyond the family to relatives and friends. The relationship between Daddy and me quickly got worse, moving from stoic to argumentative to physically abusive. I was defiant. Insensitive? Maybe. He was accusative, stubborn, and understandably hostile.

Seething anger cannot long be denied expression, nor can it do without a target. One becomes very interested when he is the chosen object of aggression. I, being the family's traditional scapegoat, was soon painted in colorful concentric circles of bull's-eye!

The sequence, a few times a week around seven-ish, would ritualistically go like this: I would have an open book, reading at the kitchen table. That, I suspect, was my first erected counter- conversational stratagem. Maybe it was a distraction. I am uncertain which, and perhaps it was both. Daddy would come and sit on the kitchen steps ready to play his part. The unwilling audience, Dolly and Pinkey, wherever in the home they happened to be, were ready too. Stage set! The play was on tonight and about to begin. No rush. Should you miss this night's performance, you may catch the encore later in the week.

"Did you hear the prime minister's speech?" he would casually begin.

I, the reluctant accomplice, unwilling to engage, would answer monosyllabically and continue so as he asked more questions. That would go on for a few minutes as he sized me up once more. I say that because his eyes would warn of his growing anger, and my apparent uncaring behavior was not helping any. Daddy was very agile. He would pounce on you before you even put up your defenses.

Well, this is where it got dangerously interesting. Whatever opinion one of us proposed, invariably the other opposed it. Inevitably! Dutifully! Ours were well-scripted roles and accommodated no straying or improvisation. Soon, he would get irate, and I, insouciant. Escalation! Intensification! Violence! Yelling! Tears. One would think we both should have learned from the last few episodes, but oh no. Never! We couldn't disappoint each other. Obligations need honor. We smoothly reversed opinions we'd vigorously espoused only recently. This was no purposeless struggle. Predictably, he would start violently slapping me around, and I would get mouthier. A few more slaps to the head and a couple of threats thrown in to spice things up would ensue. Most times, our next-door neighbor hearing the commotion, would come running over and calm us. I never hit back. Nor was I ever deprecatory or insulting. I was not afraid of him, but physical retaliation to either of my parents was a moral line I never even considered crossing, much less approached. I just did not care. Well, at the time so I thought, but having had the benefit of an objective party's estimation, I am now convinced that our physical conflict indicated much more. I had assumed the role that was necessary, that is to say, a willing scapegoat. The one punished for all the turmoil in our family at the time.

Daddy never apologized, even after he learned from Mommy's fair-weather friends that I was the least likely to have known. I guess that was how we coped with the reality of our new situation. Both of us were in terrible emotional pain, and neither of us had the foundation or the words to reach the other. I realize now that we had very different ways of facing the wreck of our family. He wanted to talk about his wife, my mother—understandable. I process and maintain my psyche by avoidance or silence mostly—a very off-putting, determined silence. He wanted to look backward; unearth and dust off past injuries; relive memories, now missed or regretted. I wanted to just let it be. He wanted validation of his redefinition of her. I wanted any place but home. He wished to debase her. I was deaf to that. After all, she was my mother, and my defense of her was as natural as sunrise. Just let it be.

Eventually, our communication became a toneless, perfunctory greeting of the day. "Good-afternoon, Daddy." And he would kind of mumble a reply with sparing eye contact. But he meant no harm or deliberate insensitivity. He was just betrayed, shamed, broken, emotionally depleted, and tired of giving of himself. Nearing the horizon of mandatory retirement, my father found that his entire life's love, toil, and anticipation were coming to this unnerving vacuousness.

Yes, we dealt with our problem differently. I started drinking and was an incipient delinquent, earnest in my search for any variety of trouble, which, fortunately, did not find me. But all I was trying to do was become a man—a "real man" with a job. Like the miners with their huge, heavy, loam-caked, dusty, scuffed, steel-tipped boots; coarse-fibered clothes and language even coarser; hard hats and boorish, ostentatious behaviors, I would become a man who could drink you under the table and still rise before dawn to be on time for work that morning. As Cecil, later on a visit home, would discover to his chagrin that I was no longer little brother. One aspires to what is perceived as valued in one's social environment. I would easily have settled for that stultifying life.

It may sometimes be complicated for a biographer of African descent to authentically write an account of him or herself or another of they own without reference to slavery. Millions of us were captured, sold, and transported across land and sea; sold again and again, while drained of intellect, labor, and very basic humanity. Wrung dry, abandoned their children in lands they never chose, without a penny, but with abundance of underserved, unrelenting disdain we could not escape. The abandonment was called emancipation, and even that drew blood; we lived with very real possibilities of re-enslavement, peonage, deportation, or genocide. Most times, corralling and isolation sufficed.

It is important to know this truth because it helps explain why my father was born with more than a fair share of deficits, and even the little chance he might have had for a life vitally lived, a life actualized, was curtailed by his cruel mulatto father. Like many blacks, I do not know of lineage beyond my father's father, and him I met once, only for a little more than a day. After our exchange of greetings, nothing more was said to me until good-bye and wishes for a safe journey home. Dennis, my brother, reports a similar experience on meeting Grandfather. He related that Grandfather observed him as if he were an unfamiliar object. Nothing I have seen or heard of my grandfather induced me to dispute Dennis' intuition in that regard.

When faced with the unknown, one ought to probe for possible reasons, rather than the easy criticism or hasty conclusions. The latter are often wrong anyway. I am also respectful of cultural mores that counsel against dishonoring or mocking parents and grandparents.

Having considered the matter, I believe that my grandfather did not know how to reach a child. He had not learned to touch fondly, lift up, play with, hug, amuse, console, encourage, or teach a young person, and he didn't know how to scold without shaming or how to communicate loving kindness and empathy with new members of another generation. By not caring for his own children, he missed those special sets of circumstances.

Not being there for bonding opportunities, he lost the chance to experience the world anew. He missed the wondrous, unforgettable, spiritual knowing of holding a young child as she observes, for the very first time, with open-mouthed awe and curiousness, a green tree bathed in early morning sunshine, leaves tantalizing shine or shadow as they move in a cool, light breeze. Then she, having learned something, becomes more intrigued and tentatively reaches out just to touch a leaf, eyes not excited but simply marveling at her discovery. She plucks a leaf and watches her own clumsy grasp and studies this new thing. Watch her! In fact, see her! See her, slack-jawed in wonderment too long, close her mouth and suck her lips. See that and be moved to moist eyes or a lump in the throat, miss such moments and, well, disinclination to engage your grandchild should surprise no one.

If the opportunity slips by—no, if it is squandered and avoided— and you never knew the tender love of a newborn soundly asleep on your chest, completely dependent on your protection, care, and nourishment, you will have missed something vital. To not experience his first grip of your pinky; the pleasure of his standing for the first time; him smiling, bright-eyed, with achievement, looking to you, always to you, for applause. That is a loss my grandfather had never grasped. You will not then remember how he would light up and run to greet your arrival home or recall that day when, sure enough of himself and of you, he no longer repeatedly looks back to ensure that you are still there, because he is now assured that you will always be there. You will not witness him freely exploring with confidence, because he knows he is loved. Having never opened your eyes, your arms, your heart to that, is it then any wonder that you welcome son's sons and daughters with a sentient, indifferent stare? Communication is learned. Caring is learned. Reciprocity is inculcated. That is your humanity.

CHAPTER XIV

IT'S ALL CONNECTED

I MENTIONED MY family's history because examining it may assist us in deciphering the reliance on physical discipline in so many of our homes and, furthermore, the effects this reality has on the chances life affords those involved in it. For hundreds of years, our ancestors lived through external controls of the self, reinforced by atrocious physical violence. That legacy is potent inter-generationally.

My grandfather's roots was traced to plantation, Greenland, which was situated in Shores Village, St. Andrew's Parrish, Barbados. Information collated from oral sources advise that Plantation Greenland's overseer, King, believed to be an Irish Caucasian, had at least three children with three women of African descent. They were two boys and a girl. One of those children was my grandfather known to us as James Henry King. His sibling brother, name uncertain, migrated to Trinidad, and there his trail ended. My grandfather, reportedly arrived in

Demerara British Guiana, from Barbados under murky circumstances and aliases.

Some believe he fled Barbados in haste, assisted by his relatives, about age twenty. My grandfather left behind a baby girl, Carlotta Walkes, now deceased, for whom he never provided anything. Nor did he make any effort to communicate with her later. In fact, they both passed away without ever seeing each other, despite being able to do so.

My grandfather, James Henry King, was about eighty years old when we met. He cried and begged my father's forgiveness … again.

We also know that he was born a shade away in time and color from the final emancipation. In British Guiana, my grandfather would have had many doors open to him. He would have been afforded opportunities denied about 95 percent of the entire population—for no reason other than his skin. He fathered Albert Edward King (Daddy). Albert's three half siblings were of another father. Albert's mother was Katherine Hazelwood, a tall, slender black woman. We called her Ma. I met her only one time. By then, she was very aged and lived with one of her daughters. Once more, Albert's father never stuck around. He must have been considered a good catch at the century's turn—six feet tall, robust, and of very light complexion. His hair must have seemed distinctly Caucasian back then. (Later, when I met him, it was just a wispy white wreath below a broad pate, burnished and freckled by time and sun.) Top it off with his skill in leatherwork—life could hardly have been kinder to him in early British Guiana.

"J. H. King, General Saddler," said the weatherworn sign on his unpainted paling at Number 2 Village, East Canje in the County of Berbice. He specialized in producing bridles, saddles, and harnesses, meeting the steady demand of sugar estates. The harnesses were used on draft mules that pulled the cane-laden punts from field to factory. The collection was called the mule train. At that time, Albert's father would have been moderately wealthy. He kept his bits, schillings, and florins in leather pouches in drawers.

When Albert was born on January 19, 1912, it is unlikely that his father welcomed him as a bundle of joy, given the fact that he hadn't lingered to parent his other child or reached out to her in anyway. It seems very likely that Albert might have been sent to him sometime later in childhood, his mother unable or unwilling to continue caring for him. It might have been the first time he, James Henry King, had been held responsible for caring for a child. His history suggests he would not have liked that at all. Rather than a bundle of joy, little Albert was surely, to him, a bundle of distress delivered to him by something other than a good-natured stork. Usually, nothing good comes of that.

From the time that Albert was born through his first tentative steps, his father may have been reading about and discussing the invasion of Libya by Italy or the crumble of the Ottoman Empire. Tectonic shifts were manifesting, power and influence being realigned. He might have been talking about the United States Marines' invasion of Honduras, Nicaragua, and Cuba or the formation of the South African National Congress by Pixley ka Isaka Seme, a Zulu graduate of Columbia University and Oxford University. Later the organization became the African National Congress led by the late President Nelson Mandela and others, some martyred. The Titanic sank just about that time too. Albert was three months old when that memorable event occurred.

Soon, equipped with a thick slate and pencil, young Albert would have been on his way to school, barefooted, legs shiny with coconut oil, walking along roads that were alternatively muddy, puddled, or dry, spiky, and rough. He would learn to read, write, and do arithmetic—just enough to succeed as a clerk in the colony. No more was expected, and no more given. A colonial plantocracy has little need for scholars, engineers, or even highly skilled workers. Basically, Albert was being taught just enough to facilitate the orderly export of sugar and alcohol to Britain and to tax unimpeded, assorted junk imported therefrom. A lack of primary education will often lead to a hard life.

Descending childhood transitions along the preferential ladder—from child, to stepchild, to invisible child, to abandoned child—is abominable, self-degrading, and cruel in its very nature. But it is not as rare as generally thought. Little Albert lived in an abusive home. His story of all that was to become of him and his thoughts of life, fairness, responsibility, love, and discipline were the elements that shaped his character there. His resilience, determination, and expectations were all forged here in his father's fiery, unforgiving home.

Oral history informs that Albert was a troubled child, and it was felt that he would do better with his father and stepmother. The details of the why and how he came to be moving between homes remain unclear. It might be that his mother was young, Albert being her first child, and she may have been unable to care for him, but what is inarguable is that nobody wanted him. His father and stepmother took him eventually.

Daddy told us that it was not a happy home, and that he was beaten severely. He admitted that he would pilfer from his father's money pouches and that he was wayward. The coins he filched he buried about the yard and often could not remember where he'd cached them. He told of one incident in which his stepmother, having caught him stealing sugar, choked him, rubbing his larynx until he expectorated blood. For another misbehavior, he was made to sleep in his father's donkey stable below the house. Young Albert shared the stable's stench, the ass's breath with flies, mosquitoes, and any crawling, nocturnal thing that harbored itself there.

That form of punishment stopped when one night, according to Daddy, he awoke to a specter of an Indian man wearing a turban and standing in the stable. He screamed his terror, ran upstairs, and burst through a window, breaking glass and crockery on his way in. That was the last time he was made to sleep there. That is what he said he saw, but a child sleeping outdoors alone in the desolate blackness of night is susceptible to imagining things so dreadful that even the turbaned Indian specter would himself scoot back to warn other ghosts that the donkey's stable was unsafe to haunt at night. That was small compared with what was to come.

Daddy's left hand was misshapen and atrophied. As young children, my siblings and I were told by our parents that he'd had an accident while working at the sugar factory. When I was about seven, he told us tearfully what had really caused the deformity. He told us only once and never again referred to it. We, when asked by curious friends, shared the sugar factory accident version. Daddy disclosed that as a preteen, he stole again from his father, who vowed it would be the last time Albert would steal from him. His father grabbed his left hand and placed it palm up on what was perhaps a meat block. With a knife he cloves deep across his son's palm. Albert bled profusely.

Time mitigates fury and uncontrolled anger. Realizing his own predicament due to the severity of Albert's injury, his father consulted with a doctor. They conspired to have him treated secretly and not report the incident to authorities. Albert was kept out of school and public eye for several weeks. The particular duration of his absence or whether his school attendance was regular after he'd healed is uncertain. What is known is that the knife's cut was so mercilessly deep that it severed the left hand's flexor muscles and tendons and caused nerve and tissue damage to the surrounding area. Mere palliative care was provided Albert on the doctor's clandestine visits, resulting in shriveling and permanent disfigurement. The hand became more and more rigid, the bones thinner and longer than those of his right hand. Instead of affecting only the area of the knife's contact, the damage extended upward above the wrist, where apparently as he grew, his fingers stretched the skin, flattened the palm, and emaciated the wrist through atrophy. That limb, from his fingertips to halfway up his forearm, was affected. The inflexible wrist was thin and hairless; the palm smooth, featureless, flat, and pale. Pardon the simile, but there is no pleasant way to accurately describe the fact of Albert's hand having the appearance and functionality of a crab's claw.

The four digits were stiff, now a single immovable unit against which his thumb may clasp an object. This hand would never, ever thread a needle or make a fist. Its owner never could become a policeman, a firefighter, or a soldier. Worse, it could never stroke or caress affectionately. His left hand was a daily reminder of a father's love denied.

Daddy needed lifelong help buttoning his right cuff. Knotting a tie was impossible. His right hand compensated by growing bigger, knuckled, and stronger.

But we've only examined the physical damage and incapacitation. The betrayal of trust, refusal of assumed protection, and the weight of being ordered to lie about the cause of his injury undoubtedly must have played havoc with his young mind. Albert might have lived in a topsy-turvy world, interpreting his father's actions as bad and yet claiming blame for what happened to him. His internal narrative would have suggested that, if he had not pinched pennies from his father, then the cut would not have happened. Albert might have regarded himself as a nuisance, worth less to his father than his donkey. He might also have thought that others perceived him in the same way. Of course, that kind of thinking is simplistic, faulty, and wrong. The consequence for appropriating a few of your father's coins is not the loss of your hand. The consequence for stealing a spoonful of sugar is not a grinding throttle. The consequence for childhood misbehavior is not banishment at night to sleep in an animal's stable.

It appears that we have here a hating father and a hated child. Where did this start? In the interim, let's ponder this, why was Albert pilfering pennies and caching the coins in holes about the yard? Are there similarities with behaviors one might identify in our household? Hint—think bread.

Our answers would likely be insecurity, anxiety, and compulsivity that found their outlet in hoarding behavior. It is not my wish to witness and memorialize this trauma passionlessly. What in heaven's name could cause a father to act so brutally toward his child? Any child? Could copious tears and countless apologies ever recompense Albert's anguish, his loss of education, trust, and childhood? Could anything return him the capabilities stifled and opportunities lost? His father was well-off financially. There was no other child in the home. What could have stoked such uncontrollable rage?

A morally empty person inevitably corrupts those about him. That is so inescapable a conclusion it might well be deemed an iron law. The application of little thought would lead one to a reasoned judgment that any of us who are forced to or choose to interact with morally corrupt or empty others will likely be corrupted. My grandfather, James Henry King, was the precipitator of the doctor's violation of his Hippocratic Oath—of his becoming coconspirator in concealment of the crime and denial of Daddy's opportunity for appropriate surgical repair that might have militated the extent of permanent physical damage. Sometimes I question whether the physician was, in fact, a Doctor of Medicine or merely a well-compensated quack. No one could ever know the extent of psychological harm that was wreaked on Albert, and then neglected.

I know that Daddy had not healed from the traumatic events of his childhood. This I believe to be true, intuitively, because of the following: As young kids, we—Dolly, Pinkey, and I—used to run to greet his arrival from work about five o'clock every evening. Even neighbors' kids joined the greeting party. He used to merrily lift the girls, the neighbor's kids too, high above his head in fond play. I ran with them but would walk beside him as he swung, lifted, laughed, and played with them on the street while walking joyously home. He never acknowledged me, but I went, nevertheless. One day, desiring to feel included, I held his left hand, the maimed one, as we walked, whereupon he instantly became cross, glared, and roughly pulled his hand away, even adding words of rejection. I never touched his left hand again, but my compassion never left.

Daddy informed us that he ran away from home at a young age. This must have been during mid-adolescence. He met and befriended a crafty older boy named Nathan, who died some years prior to this writing. The two boys survived as runaways do. Nathan was an incorrigible burglar, and Albert soon became the lookout—at least once, we were told, but given their needs, I suspect more. Their actions might have been inspired by the pursuit of excitement rather than motivated by need, perhaps both. Daddy recounted to us a late-night venture to purloin property from an occupied house in Berbice. It was Nathan's idea, and of course Daddy trailed along. "It was pitch-black," Daddy said. They waited, hidden among bushes, from which concealment they observed the household make ready for bed. When all was quiet, Nathan made the entry but was soon discovered. A hue and cry followed. Neighbors joined the chase, but neither fleet- footed miscreant was caught. Daddy described their flight from the premises. He remembered being urged by Nathan, "Run, run,

Butta, run!" as they made swift their way in the darkness and thick bush near the seashore. Like I said, it might not have been a singular incident, but life has this queer obsession with choice and consequences. The latter follows the former as reliably as night follows day. Free will, some philosophers say. Within permitted social parameters, I add. We may also agree that one's next step is trailed to the last. Nathan and Albert could have continued the thrill of the chase, from which no good could come to anyone, or they could take the other narrower, more challenging road. Daddy chose to find work as a helper at a bakery. He made bread and sweet rolls primarily—skills that saved him from the street and served him well in our home later on in his life. The two friends gradually drifted apart. Now and then they had a chance encounter. But Nathan chose the facile road that led inexorably to the prison door. Daddy said he never saw or heard of Nathan again after that door closed.

That might have been the root lesson of Daddy's favorite allegory which I'll tell in his honor. A discontented, fun-seeking pet parrot thought he should join the adventurous others in an afternoon raid on a farmer's fruits. All were having a jolly skylark, feasting unfettered among the trees, flitting in the sun, amusing themselves, and loving it up until ... well, the farmer suddenly arrived armed with a gun and put an immediate end to the entertainment. Guess who got shot? The experienced regulars flew speedily away. They were practiced at the art of escape. The pet parrot got back to his cage alone but mortally wounded. "Bad company, the parrot said," my father would conclude dramatically, "as the bird slowly laid down his head and died."

Most of what Daddy taught us was conveyed through aphorisms and basic storytelling. In his lighter moods, he told myths of Brer Anansi, a mythical trickster God of West African culture. Anansi seems to be the equivalent of Loki, trickster deity in the pantheon of Greek and Roman culture. We laughed again and yet some more when we retold the stories. He spoke of the houri and the conga fish, a story that taught about reliability and credulity. He animated stories by use of oral traditions, teaching through the voices of animals.

I know that Daddy loved his family, since he evinced most signs of happiness when we were all together in our small living room-cum dining room-cum bedroom. That's when he was most affectionate and lighthearted. Then would also be the time when Dolly and Pinkey, having equipped themselves with combs, brushes, and pomade, would seize upon his head, comb and braid his receding hair. Sometimes they got creative and gave him the side sweep and tried curls. In fact, they did whatever they wished with his hair. That, cueing from his gentle countenance and repose, must have given him the greatest gratification. Yes, those were happy times. His other side, his alter ego was in those moments unveiled. I remember drawing a portrait of him then, and the family loved it. But storytelling time was so interesting.

Mommy would throw in her stories as well. A favorite was "peas and rice and pork for dinner," an inadvertent revelation of wrongdoing. "The gifts of eggs from the poor, old woman with sores on her back" taught values of kindness to elders and compassion for the sick. Once broken, the eggs' gifts were determined by the degree of empathy that had been shown to the old, afflicted, fantastical woman.

She told stories too of the dead and of spirits. We learned about the "Ol' Higue" a fiery vampire myth (probably linguistically corrupted from Old Hag and known as the Soucouyant in parts of Caribbean mythology) and "the Moon Gazer," an exceptionally tall, slender, gossamer-like apparition, which, in the wee hours, stood unmoving, legs spread across a street, and well, you guessed it, stared fixedly at the moon. One walks through the Moon Gazer's legs at his or her peril. These were scary stories to a kid, not unlike campfire tales. I was puzzled as to how the gazer occupied himself when the moon was in the waning phase of the lunar cycle.

The mythical Massacurraman lived in the dark rivers and snatched the unwary, drowning them in the waters beneath. Though it was never known to have devoured anyone, the bodies, according to the teller, were never found. Maybe it was just a prankster Massacura-teen gone rogue. Who knows? Some swore this creature had been seen a few times—usually by someone else's cousin, who was alone when he saw it. He told the teller's friend's brother, who had never been known to tell a lie. The legendary creature remained as remote and solitary as the Loch Ness Monster but not as benign. (No, Dominique, my grand-daughter, Mommy did not say whether Massacuraman had a wife.)

Mommy's stories were sometimes mirthful but often frighteningly enjoyable, until bedtime, that is. None of us wanted to be first in the bedroom. Presumably, the abominable thing might leave its riverine lair to come all the way over to get just us at our house, in our beds. This despite him not reported to be amphibious or ambulant. But folkloric beings are known to be capable of anything; just ask the Greeks, Egyptians, Eastern Europeans, and Ethiopians of antiquity.

Mommy's tales were delivered with suitable emotion and a knack for morbidity. I remember well the one that had the preacher descending his stairway singing, "Dinner for One" (Please Jane) (a la Nat King Cole's ballad involving James). The preacher had just murdered his wife in their bedroom. His housekeeper just happened to be named Jane, according to Mommy.

The one that gave me goose bumps was the tale of the 3:00 a.m. ghost, who walked the dark road singing, "The way is dark, and I am far from home." This was probably a deliberate modification or misquotation of the poem, "The Way Is Dark and Home Is Far Away."

Asked why the ghost didn't just head home while there was still time, rather than walking the same circles every night, our resident folklorist explained that he must have done something really bad and not confessed his sin.

Ah, but it was fun. Both parents were at home having a great time talking freely with their family.

It is known that Mommy and Cecil "saw things." There could be something to it; I don't know. I have never experienced an apparition. But neither am I aligned with the skepticism of others who refuse to appreciate that the experiences were real to the observers. I am open enough to know that, if two or more people who have never conversed on the subject are able to describe consistently particular phenomena in terms of time, place, appearance, and behavior, the existence of said phenomena is worth further consideration.

On the other hand, I do concede that a fear-filled mind can create phantasms that only one person experiences, as well as the possibility of mass hysteria. Another Cecil-classic can demonstrate just such occasion.

My father brought a huge, industrial spool previously used to coil power cables. The spool had been discarded by the company, and he thought it a fine idea to bring it home for the kids to ride. It was still dusk when he placed it below the house. Cecil, at that time, was out to the movies, where he was being entertained by Creature from the Black Lagoon. In strict adherence to the horror genre, the big, black, scaly, finned, fish-faced amphibian of manly attributes had a predilection for blond, scantily clad, helpless young women, superlatively talented for piercing screams and lithe fainting.

On his way home well after dark, his malleable imagination sufficiently massaged by the movie, Cecil perceived the spool in the shadows and, from that, conjured a hulking monster. His problem was how to get upstairs to the house without his legs being grabbed, for each time he mustered courage and moved closer to the stairs, the monster grew closer too. When he retreated, the monster withdrew to the deeper shadows. Cecil now had a dilemma for which he chose a temporary solution—he would remain where he was, on the road, out of reach of the creature that menaced him. So there he paced the road as it grew later and later, watching the monster watch him, believing it was determined to get him. His mind closed to all other options, Cecil decided to make a sprint for it, figuring he would get to the open front door in one giant leap before the monster could reach through the stairs and pull him under.

Meanwhile, in the living room, where the rest of the family had gathered, our attention was captured by a long, strident scream, accompanied by the sound of feet running up the stairs. And suddenly, there was Cecil, prone on the floor, wide-eyed, confused, and blowing like a horse. It took some time to calm him and explain away his fear. Then of course we laughed.

CHAPTER XV

A FINER SIDE

DADDY WAS USUALLY melodramatic, gauged from the stories he told and the things that gave him pleasure. Among his favorite songs was "If You Were the Only Girl in the World and I Was the Only Boy," made popular by Doris Day and Gordon MacRae through the movie, By the Light of the Silvery Moon. I remember him singing it for us one night in the kitchen. He loved the mellow entreaties of South Pacific and Showboat, as well as the classical instrumentals broadcast on the radio early Sunday mornings.

When Gone With The Wind and Imitation of Life screened, he took Mommy to see both. He loved maudlin movies but also favored those of political genre, like Judgment at Nuremberg and, most notably, The Manchurian Candidate.

Daddy's favorite poem, which he often wove into his long lectures, was "For Want of a Nail." He was an earnest believer in the incontrovertible justice of time; his maxim was, "God's mill grinds slow, but it grinds fine." Sometimes he dragged the word fine, simultaneously rubbing his thumb and forefinger, as one would to test granular quality. Here again, we see by inference his passion for due punishment—now or later. Never known to set foot in any church, despite two being within a five and ten-minute walk, he respected religion and sent us to church. He bought the Catholic Standard and other publications of the kind. Daddy was a steadfast listener to evangelicals, particularly Reverend Oral Roberts and Reverend Billy Graham. After sessions of "Armageddon" and another of "The World Tomorrow," he joined in silent prayer by placing his hand on the radio as asked by the preacher. He donated his time and labor to install plumbing when the Catholic Church needed to build a two-story annex for teaching and recreational purposes. We, the boys, all volunteered labor for the project.

The long serving priest, Father Hale, visited our home sometimes for a chat. He was always graciously welcomed. Father Hale was a short, middle-aged, introspective man. We went to the Catholic Church regularly, mostly Dennis, Cecil, and I. We were all altar boys. I carried the boat (brass container for the incense crystals) and was second server and once first server, the latter for a 6:00 a.m. Mass, thank God for the sparse attendance, for I was very nervous. On Saturday mornings, about a dozen of us boys swept the church; polished the brass; and cleaned candlesticks, the altar, and such.

The girls were not as regular, but all of us children were present for baptism, confession, confirmation, and First Communion. The latter two even a minimally practicing Catholic never forgets. We all wore white and had formal breakfast with the priest. Novena, Lent, Good Friday, and Easter were vital in our lives. If ever there were a day, I felt closest to happiness for no apparent reason, it was immediately after Easter Sunday Mass. The rituals, the hymns and prayers, the fresh flowers and burning candles and frankincense vapors—all gave rise to such pleasing sensations that stirred the spirit. On the other hand, if ever there were a day I dreaded, it was Good Friday.

The protracted, wearisome, mind-numbing monotony of Mass in Latin would tempt even a staunch parishioner to prostrate himself in the aisle, bawl, and sob piteously, "Please! Enough! I beg of you. Let me go home!

Our Good Friday Mass was scheduled for 3:00 p.m. That didn't help any, due to the facts that it became hotter with so many people in the church and the required all-day fasting until 6:00 p.m.

CHAPTER XVI

LISTEN AND LEARN

DADDY LOVED THE news. He read newspapers most evenings and compulsively on Sunday. Not a casual reader by nature, he would sit and read newspapers from beginning to end. He was not drawn to the sensational. His main interest was politics. Sometimes after work he would have chats with Mr. Benjamin, a longtime neighbor who lived at the third apartment from us. Daddy called him Benjie and respected his opinions. I suppose that listening to their discussions got me interested in reading and politics too. It was to later strike me as odd that they "followed" the news—that is, in a passive, negative sense. But that was their world. Colonized and oppressed people evidence a psychology of powerlessness and reverence for the oppressor.

Through Daddy and Benjie's conversations I learned about the Nuremberg trials. I learned about race in a different way when they were discussing Ian Smith's intrepid "Unilateral Declaration of Independence of Rhodesia." A White minority ruled the British colony in Southern Africa. The move dared the British to act and underlined the obvious—that the sun had indeed set on the British Empire.

Mr. Benjie's opinion was that nothing would be done by the British, even though Ian Smith had committed treason by declaring independence, a capital crime. That position was quite pragmatic, and subsequent events proved him correct. On the other hand, Daddy seriously believed the contrary. He expressed that the British had no choice than to invade militarily, put Smith on trial, and hang him on conviction. Daddy's nature was conservative and ruled by law and order. Thus, his argument was aligned with his personality and his situation. Was he naive? In the particular instance, absolutely! For the sake of his descendants, let's make a small divergence.

It was on the same back stairs that I first learned of the Mau Mau rebellion. The press branded the Mau Mau terrorists and reported they were committing unspeakable crimes against the British settlers. Today we know quite the opposite was true. I authored an article entitled "Colonial History ... The Mau Mau Resistance Movement" and posted it to a website called BlueGadfly (bluegadfly.com) on November 11, 2013. Below is an extended version of that piece.

I would not have known about the Mau Mau fighters had it not been for the discussions my father and a neighbor used to have at our tenement's backyard. The press reports described the Mau Mau as terrorist.

Earlier this week, the British government finally confessed in court that they committed atrocities, apologized, and agreed to compensate the Mau Mau veterans and others who suffered torture and other violence.

The movement began in 1952 and lasted about eight years. Basically, it was an armed struggle to regain their land and other rights dispossessed them by the British. Africans were forcibly removed from their prime farmlands and herded into concentration camps.

Torture was common and savage. Lives, not worth the cost of a bullet. The brutality was so heinous, the casualties so disproportionate and lopsided, that Sir Winston Churchill, then prime minister of the United Kingdom had to ask the British military commander if he could not achieve the same ends "without having to kill so many of them."

Just in case you think Churchill had pangs of conscience, rethink that. His expressed concern was that the slaughter not be known to the House of Commons, and with the daily killings and unspeakable torture, he feared discovery.

The Mau Mau was of the Kikuyu tribe. It is estimated that 11,500 Mau Mau were killed and about 480,000 imprisoned. Over one million Kenyans were held in military enclosed villages. About 2,000 others who did not align with the Mau Mau died. Less than 100 settlers were killed. This was pretty standard expropriation. This was in my time, in the time of Stevie Wonder and Queen Elizabeth II. The surviving victims may get about six thousand dollars (US) each.

Just for clarity and to ensure everyone reading understands, we are talking about concentration camps in Africa in 1952. That is subsequent to the Nazi concentration camps and the later Nuremberg trials of 1945–1946. That was after the notorious Japanese concentration camps and enslavement of other Asians and prisoners of war and the Japanese-American concentration camps (though we preferred to call ours interment facilities).

Is this not all outrageous? Do we have an issue of widespread naiveté? Well, there is troublesome, well-researched, and published literature about what happens to the minds of oppressed people. I will summarize for brevity.

People under dominance and dependency cannot help mimicking the oppressor, valuing the bully above themselves, even when their very own existence is under threat by the oppressor.

Now and then a firebrand revolutionary emerges, who, awakened, see the fictitiousness very clearly, but more often than not, the result proves to be merely another pantomime of Plato's Cave. Neither the oppressed nor the oppressor easily breaks the cycle. It all ends up a ridiculous, tragic performance. But there are always other means, more tolerable to the world and the victims themselves, of achieving the same ends—ghettoization! Every race suffered that at one time or another. Most would not see or understand it.

So, to come back to Daddy's worldview, it is quite normal that he would align himself with the British, so to speak, and vocalize his view that Smith must be punished. From Daddy, I acquired an interest in politics and self-understanding, which shaped my own consciousness. I'd like to refer you to a relevant article I wrote about participating in your own debasement. I see it every single day. Pinkey liked the piece and asked that I include it. In, "Retrieve Your Mind," I wrote on July 24, 2014:

Suppose you were asked to tell your story to your grandchildren. What would you say before boring them to death? Would it not be best to capture your time and relate the good and bad to them, discretion adjusted to their ages? Few lives are that compelling without interspersed embellishments. Come on, we don't have all day. Their eyes might start rolling anytime now, like they have seasickness or some similar affliction. You have to give them something they can reflect on—something lessons can be drawn from, and in a culturally relevant context, a story with a thread. For me I'll tell them about the yard fowl.

In the regional dialect of the Caribbean, a yard fowl is literally a chicken raised naturally. They peck around and are easy to raise. No, they hadn't yet graduated to "organic" or "free range" Well, excuse me, but don't insult my yard fowl, they are colorful, sinewy, disease- resistant survivors! and the cocks crow! The yard fowl is conditioned by a three-day restraint, a fettered foot would do, and feeding, so that they will remain in the bounds of the owner's property and will not later leave, though quite free to do so. Dependency is created.

Extrapolated, it is very easy to see the metaphor of servile, exploitative human relationships.

In postcolonial political discourse, yard fowl, is a slur with connotations synonymous with "Uncle Tom", in the United States. The most publicized insult I can recall followed its use in a Barbados Parliamentary debate turned acrimonious. The yard fowl. (granddaughter Naija, it had nothing to do with whether the bird liked the owner)

Lest you think that I grew up "enlightened", every generation faces this in some form of conditioning. You and I are no different. My parents were no different, nor were theirs. I grew up on Tarzan, cowboys and Indians, World War II White heroes, Superman, King Kong, and other conveyances of mass miseducation. We absorbed the movies, comic books, religion, and countless other forms of media-purveyed racist crap, and paid our own hard-earned money to be further miseducated. The games we played, in full supervision of all adults, caricatured others. Genocidal wars were portrayed in role reversal everywhere. It was total brainwash, deliberately and profitably disguised as entertainment—veneration of the oppressor, conformity with his desires, and mimicking his values and deceptions. That we did not see!

Before you opine, know that it was a Black, popular calypso singer of the Caribbean who created and sang "Congo Man" and we danced. It did not matter that the record album was marketed with the singer sporting a spear, a bleached bone in his nose, and painted grinning face; a necklace of teeth complemented other adornments on his bare, black, sweaty chest. It did not matter that primitive, guttural expressions interwoven throughout the lyrics extolled the good fortune of African "head-hunters" encountering two White women, lost in the jungle. The salacious narrative continued with language intertwining rape, cunnilingus and cannibalism. Reinforcement of racial preference and self-hatred were so obvious to any clear-thinking adult. Yet, nobody seemed offended, nobody objected, and nobody made him do it. It was a top seller, and we danced! Oh, how we danced, danced, and danced!

The complete mind-body domination by the British also caused denial of reality, sycophantic reasoning that in turn led to so-called "free will" actions, inimical to one's own economic and social interests. Evidence the coronation of Queen Elizabeth II, latest in a line of English monarchs. Though the momentous ceremony, the theatrics of aristocracy, was taking place in England, thousands of miles away, Mommy and Daddy joined the throngs who travelled at their great expense of time and money to British Guiana's capital, for the festivities. Distilleries marketed special blends of rum, and we of course, paid more for the label. Extra transport schedules ensured timely travel to the city to celebrate the occasion, so momentous to a population under oppression of the very colonial power and personages being celebrated. The merchants feasted on the revelers. Spirits flowed, spirits soared as all sang "Rule Brittania" and the anthem, "God Save the Queen". Incredible! Absolutely incredible! One would think it comical were the dynamics of dominance not understood.

The above does not in any way assert inferiority of intellect, in fact, the absurdity is consequential to preponderancy in the colonial world where the oppressed praise and imitate the oppressor, while thanking her/him for their beneficence. The centuries-old anthem, "Rule Britania" includes the phrase "Britons never ever shall be slaves". We, the children of slaves, still under colonial rule, a few generations removed— only ninety years had passed since the Emancipation Act—we so celebrated and proudly sang. There is good reason for pageantry. It is mesmeric and subtle, but make no mistake, it is not benign. That was my time. We were the good yard fowls.

This time is now yours. What is going on now, quite blatantly, that you do not see? Sensual women undress on stage and camera for money they do not need, fame they cannot keep, and youth they cannot retain. The less connected or endowed twerk and climb monkey-poles. Our debased youth revel in violent, prurient, misogynistic, self-loathing entertainment of any licentious varieties possible. Black women are stuffed into for-profit jails with no tomorrow while their men are shot in the street like dogs, mostly by their brothers, often by the police. We tacitly approve the bullying of the poor and walk away from our commitments and fidelity, leaving our children to the scavengers and enslavers of the street- the vultures of the vulnerable. Do you see that? Would you care even if you understood why?

Phenomena do not occur in a vacuum, my dears. Look for causality or at least contributive elements. Yours is of a generation better educated; free (mostly) inexhaustible information is but a click away. Yet the lazy, powerless, self-sapping mantra, of nobody told me, persists. What shiny, overpriced playthings; unneeded accoutrements; and banal, self-despising messages in the guise of entertainment, distract? How did we ever get so poor, idiotic, and callous in every sense, beginning with our own self-regard? All of us are susceptible; most are complicit and obsequious. All of us are responsible for fulfilling simple moral duties, to protest flagrant, unconscionable injustice and to uphold values of decent citizenship.

Today, credibility is not attributed unless there is scholarly support. Well, you learn best by getting information for yourself. Be voracious, be earnest about your education; and don't allow space for what is not best for you. Be passionate, not passive. There are thousands of free, uncrowded libraries in the United States. You do not need an interlocutor. Read classical literature and world history as a start. With diligence, you will grow intellectually and spiritually to crave other serious works; get to know and do what's in your best interests.

So, now, my dears, now that your lenses might have been wiped just a bit, I hope you unlearn what has been deliberately taught for generations and develop consciousness apposite to your time. Remember there is always someone in charge and that person is you!

CHAPTER XVII

HE PLAYED WITH FIRE TOO

IN THE RADIO, he had to "catch" the BBC World News at noon. Daddy loved geopolitics. His sympathies more often lay with the British and the Americans than with emerging nations breaking from Colonial rule. I can see him now, in his work clothes and big safety boots standing beside the polished Grundig radio on the shelf in our living room. The newscaster announces dispassionately, "For the fifth consecutive day, American B-52 bombers pounded North Vietnam … Heavy casualties on both sides … The Mekong Delta … And in Cambodia …"

When it was over at 12:15 p.m., he would hasten off to work. Albert Edward King was an enigmatic individual—a quiet man, usually sitting alone and pensive. At those times, his head would be slightly bowed and tilted to the right. His legs would be slightly outstretched and his hands clasped between his knees. His shoulders sometimes slump just a little. One might discern some contentment but could never be definitive about his happiness. He would sit like that for a about an hour after work and then rise with an audible sigh. Our father may be correctly described as patient, passive, and slow to anger. But it might also be true to portray him as a seemingly quiet, intolerant, smoldering man, slow to act. This may be deduced from his apparent melancholy and the suddenness of his verbal or physical attacks, disproportionate to the cause of his vexation.

His was an unshakeable commitment to his union, British Guiana Mineworkers Union (BGMWU). He protested and struck in consort with his fellow wage earners and, like they did, loathed scabs. But he did not particularly care for wildcat strikes and disregarded their calls. He regularly attended union meetings at their hall on Powell Crescent, obliquely situated a few hundred yards from the market and the river. When needed, especially for essential, high-attendance meetings, open-air gatherings were held in the public park near both buildings. Usually a podium, microphone, and amplifiers were in place on a temporary platform. Passersby would pause and gaze at the loud rally or merely observe while walking to or from the market. Taking notice was unavoidable.

BGMWU hall was an aluminum and green, sturdy structure elevated about five steps from the ground and abutting the road. Its prominence derived from large, rectangular pillars at the front and a fairly large patio ushering to two wide, double-doored entrances. Inside, one could appreciate smooth; well-finished hardwood floors; big jalousie windows; and an imposing stage for meetings, bands, performances, and such entertainment. Restrooms were off to the right near an anteroom, the latter available for manifold purposes. The hall's cream and green interior was always well maintained by a diligent caretaker.

Sturdy and prominent as its edifice was the union's strength as a national political force. It was well organized and capable of crippling strikes, the most memorable and successful being the 180-day strike. So much in solidarity was Daddy that he placed himself at risk of everything. Support for that estimation stems from a series of occurrences at home and in public space.

A fundamental political realignment in the making was apparent—one that promised prodigious opportunities for wealth and upward social mobility to locals. Sometime around 1959, preparations were being made for independence from Britain. But mineworkers were demanding what they always did—increased pay and better working conditions. This time, however, the demands included pension payments. The Bauxite Company balked. Subsequent negotiations seemed moribund despite assistance from the labor department. The company appeared intransigent, while workers questioned the probity and motives of their elected representatives. Inertia and shaken confidence spawned rumors and restlessness. This was an unpropitious time to hold a public meeting, especially if one chose to stand on a platform under a tree. But the union did anyway, to their later dismay.

Daddy was among the crowd of hundreds. He held aloft a conspicuous, green placard with red lettering proclaiming workers' demands. The day before, he'd had me make it for him.

The union's longtime president, pseudonym Wilistone, a very dark, podgy little man unremarkable of bearing or confidence, was by pure chance positioned encircled by his frowning audience. A few were sitting on their bicycles toward the back. With his prepared speech becoming less and less persuasive, the audience soon transformed to a rowdy, heckling mob. Try as he might, his words were ineffectual in lowering the noticeable tension. Truth be told, some folks were just plain disagreeable. Insults and threats were hurled. Emotions soared hot and high. "Traitor!" "Sellout!" These and worse were yelled from the midst of the now implacable crowd.

A word of advice to the young reader: Among every pre- riotous crowd, there is at least one fool—one useless fool with kindling and nothing but devilment of volition. An angry, heckling crowd, soon to be mob, is putty in his hands. Our fool shouted, "Hang him!"

Immediately, the cry resonated about, whipping the crowd. Yes, and as opportunity would have it, there was the hapless president already standing on a platform under the reachable bough of a burly tree; and my father, was there too, abetting by presence and excited by the scene.

The suddenness with which the rope was delivered was alarmingly. A noose was expeditiously contrived, and the word was fast becoming deed. Held immobile by the mob, President Willistone soon found the noose looped around his short, chubby, sweating neck, the rope's other end thrown across a thick bough, ready to be drawn taut.

But for the providential arrival of an armed police party, the poor, shaken man would surely have been lynched, given the collective mindlessness of the miscreants.

It may well be that the crowd intended to do no more harm than to scare and perhaps even bully the president into working effectively in their representation at the negotiating table. Who knows? But in a crowd, emotions obscure good judgment. The individual's identity is subordinated to collective inspiration and reinforces the mass. That's when very regrettable deeds are manifest.

But, in this case, no harm was done, though strictly speaking laws were broken—a most regrettable deed did not come to fruition. Daddy, like many in the crowd, was not legally responsible, not criminally culpable. But he and others were undoubtedly found wanting, the least of which being of empathy. It would have been prudent to leave, having observed the lawlessness and potent exuberance of their peers. Moreover, any among that crowd could have yelled dissent, but all chose to do nothing but witness amusedly.

Another incident occurred soon after that led me to conclude that Daddy enjoyed a spectacle, that his identity was easily absorbed by a crowd, and that he was latently predisposed to violence. On this occasion, he assembled with a group of workers infuriated over the union's perceived lackadaisical process in delivering on workers' expressed concerns. Again!

It was a little after 4:30 p.m., bright and dusty, the end of the normal workday for most employees. There was a bustle about. Some folks were trying to get to the first show at the Crescent Cinema, others to the market for snacks, produce, and such victuals or to small ferryboats plying the slow in-tide of the Demerara River. Some were making their way to a liquor purveyor's place of merriment, and still others were just heading home, tired. It was in the midst of these activities that Daddy and cohorts chose to step up their protest, which rapidly escalated to intimidation and grew more extreme from there.

The union officials prudently retreated to and locked themselves in a small, wooden building adjacent to the union hall. The flat, three-room building sat at the juncture of Arvida Road and Powell Crescent, the town's business center. Roofed with wood and galvanized aluminum and ventilated by slatted windows, this refuge was selected for urgency, certainly not for impregnability. But it sufficed at least to delay the angry mob's access to the cowering officials within. And guess who was among the two dozen or so culprits of havoc? Yes, our father, and now not merely a passive witness. He was in the midst of the angry bunch, exercising all the menace and disorderliness they could muster. My dad, the authoritarian at home, my father, an otherwise quiet man, was a boisterous participant aided by two other men ripping out the window slats, scaring people. I ache for the fear those trapped innocents must have experienced. That too he thought funny.

The police were local and had good leadership. Assessing the disturbance as more bravado than anything wicked, they easily contained the situation, more or less just shooing the assailants away. Order restored. No one was arrested or prosecuted. Thus was the power of the company and the union. They, the powers that be, had no interest in any punitive action, judicial or otherwise. Paramount were conducive labor relations and production. Countrywide publicity of labor unrest and strikes at the mining company were unwanted.

My father, fallible like all of us, made ridiculous errors of judgment, exercised deficient personal restraint, and behaved in ways that placed others in fear for their safety. His own actions could have had tragic consequences. It is unacceptable to take refuge in the often expressed, "I made a mistake." Nothing here presented legal, ethical, or moral ambiguity. Mere application of basic common sense and minimal self-control would have sufficed. Negative examples are, in many cases, just as instructive, powerful, and enduring as deliberate teaching of duty, expectations, and good citizenship. Every action causes another and yet another. I took from my father the precept of self-mastery, meaning you first control your thoughts and the emotions that stem from them. All actions begin with a thought. Absent self-mastery, nefarious thoughts would find rich, fertile ground to take root and fly you about whichever way the wind blows. Unbridled emotions cause actions, many times lamentable. Let's suppose the fortunate parts of the events had not occurred. For example, let's imagine that the arrival of the police was not instant, and the players were less forgiving. My father, among others, might have been charged criminally, tossing away their freedom for punishment. And that's just one of a series of detrimental cascades that might have concluded either of the events. Daddy placed his family in jeopardy of serious financial ruin. He certainly could have lost his job. Concomitantly, his wife and their children would no doubt, have soon been homeless, subjected to the harshness that a tumble further down the social-economic slope immediately attends. All of this leads back to Daddy's faulty thinking and frail self-management, but he still thought it funny. Yes, he played with fire and taunted calamity, but he remains my father. The incidents related here do not amount to condemnation of his life.

CHAPTER XVIII

WOULD SOMEONE PLEASE RAISE THE ADULTS

THROUGH MY FATHER'S eyes, I was lucky to experience how swiftly one's situation could change—how catastrophically! There are some things that industry, thrift, and foresight may protect us against; others, well, one rolls with the punches. Impish life perversely loves astonishment and distress.

One little understood life challenge is the dubious blessing of sudden wealth acquisition. It buffets your boat just as turbulently as its sister, the precipitous departure of prosperity. Sages, and of course friends, repeatedly tutor on the flight of fortune, but few counsel on the trials of swift, unexpected enrichment. Either circumstance necessitates fundamental changes in how we think, what we think, what we do, where we choose to go, and how we relate to others and they to us. Realignment of power, deference, duty, status, communication—every single aspect of our connectedness is affected in some way, for better or worse. But never, never again will exist the status quo, we do, where we choose to go, and how we relate to others and they to us. Realignment of power, deference, duty, status, communication—every single aspect of our connectedness is affected in some way, for better or worse. But never, never again will exist the status quo.

I begin with the given aphorism that, in a gold rush, the miner's lot is seldom improved. The first truth is that few find much of anything valuable. With hope grounded in a belief in luck, the miner misplaces his faith, convinced that the next dig might be the big dig, as he drains his life away chasing an elusive dream. The second is that there are too many greedy, people arriving to take advantage of him. They make a living off his strenuous endeavors, stealing his scarce food just short of his mouth and selling it back to him, always for much more. They rob his growth and dampen his aspirations, nullifying any good fortune that comes his way. And they never cease until he is irredeemably pauperized, if not sucked dry and dead.

Daddy never seemed to be caught up in excessive dialogues about right and wrong and exceptions. Daddy lived by simple maxims and shared his wisdom, a gift of experience, as appropriate to the occasion—little gems of sagacity. For instance, he believed that the probabilities of living without encountering adversity of some kind, sometime are in no one's favor. Thus, he was a saver, always wary of his rainy day. For the want of a nail; wasteful woe makes woeful want; don't count your chickens before they're hatched. Remember, though, that he was born into World War I, raised provincially, endured difficulties of World War II, and had close acquaintance with penury from adolescence until permanent work with DEMBA lifted him economically.

Excuse my short digression, it is needed to explain the milieu in which my father provided for his family and cared for us, in weather fair or foul. This protection and sustenance he gave unstintingly. But for his steadfast shepherding, this homage might not have been possible, let alone sincere.

The company had obtained a 999-year lease to thousands of acres of land about sixty-five miles up the Demerara River— on both banks. To get to the location, one would travel south from the coastal Capital, Georgetown. In the early days the area was completely dependent on "the steamer," moniker for the white-painted triple-decker, christened MV RH Carr. She was the vital link to Georgetown, offering postal services along the way to sparse villages and picking up and depositing produce and passengers on journeys to and fro. The lower deck, called second-class, accommodated mostly hucksters, other itinerant peddlers, and thrifty men. A portion below the weather deck was set aside for cattle on their last journey, fresh fish packed in ice, fresh fruit, and sundry necessities for the town.

In the vessel's early service, the middle deck, referred to as first-class, was a promenade deck and a full-service, à la carte restaurant, complete with flatware and white tablecloths. Lunch by reservation. Mommy often ate there and spoke of it in highly complementary terms. But the owners soon thought that an open liquor bar was profitable, most needed, and did the necessary conversion.

The uppermost deck—the captain's deck—permitted a small number of the very important travelers. It remains mysterious as to how one got included in the privilege of exclusion—what fare they paid for the pleasure of literally, and figuratively, I might add, looking down on the bustling ordinary folk, like us, who made the whole enterprise profitable.

Three factors had coalesced to develop the area: (1) Survey samples indicated large deposits of high-grade bauxite. (2) Demand was unusually high for aluminum, the core ingredient of which is metal-grade bauxite. (3) The location of the bauxite was in a British Colony.

Aluminum's atypical importance was related to the need for thousands of warplanes and sundry materiel for war and reconstruction. Labor, though, was not immediately available for the heavy industrial infrastructure required for mining. Thus, technical and managerial staff expatriated from Canada. Subordinate labor needed to be enticed from coastal residences to the heavily forested site. That problem had been solved by offering high wages.

No other entity was comparable. In McKenzie, one could quadruple his income, the work was steady, and the longevity of such prospects was perceived to be excellent. Men, especially of African descent, had left farms, cattle, and paddy fields in favor of wage labor. Demand was so strong, recruitment so successful that folks migrated from Barbados, St. Lucia, Grenada, St. Vincent, and other islands of the Eastern Caribbean in search of work.

Needed were surveyors, heavy-duty clearing and excavation machine operators, masons, carpenters, welders, laborers, medical workers, sanitation workers, locomotive engineers, and every other laborer imaginable to develop a small, industrial city in remote, pristine land. It was a powerful magnet. Given that the mining and ore treatment were fostered in a colonial economy, urban planning and human development interests were not high on anyone's to-do list. I doubt seriously that social and environmental impact studies were ever done. So the stage was set and the bet made. It was time to roll the dice.

Men went to McKenzie, leaving their families behind with promises that they would reunite later. Sometimes the men would promise to go home on weekends, common in the world of migrant labor. These fathers, sons, and brothers came especially from West Berbice, Buxton, and West Bank Demerara. That city folks weren't much interested would be a fair conjecture.

The company built several long, wooden, single-story buildings. Elevated on stilts, the buildings each had entrances at the front and back. A long aisle, about five feet wide, connected the two doorways. On either side of the passageway were small rooms, seemingly intended to house one man in each. But the need quickly outpaced the supply. It was common for three or four men to share a room. At one end of each structure were commodes and showers. There were no kitchens with appliances, though each building had a small room with sinks, cupboards, and counters. All of this suggested the buildings' inhabitants needed to make other arrangements for cooking. The more frugal residents used small, one-burner electric plates to prepare meals in their rooms, ventilated by jalousie windows—minimalism at its very best. These boot camp-like buildings were known as the bachelors' quarters.

We called them BQ. Soon they became notorious for various transgressions and excesses.

Opportunities for female employment were constrained and discriminatory. One struggles to discover a reason the company would not hire women in jobs of any kind other than the small administrative office. Under the circumstances, some women took in lunch-only boarders. Even that was beset with problems of marital faithfulness. Others opened stalls in the market, and from there, they sold snacks, cakes, and beverages. But most remained at home maintained by their male partners.

The social crisis came imperceptibly, but came it did with destructive force, its energy drawn from incredible imbalance in gender and age distribution. Compounding the unfortunate situation was the fact that most of the upper Demerara population had not known each other previously. No strong neighborhood or kinship bonds had yet developed. Soon prostitutes arrived, perfidy their bosom friend. Since faithlessness and fidelity cannot abide, fidelity quietly departed less robust families. But that kind of entertainment gets old quickly and needs continual refreshing. The gamblers, thieves, peddlers of needless junk and other ne'er- do-wells arrived like moths to a flame. Vultures to the weak might be a more apt metaphor. Wanting shelter from sunlight, these curs idled their time until darkness invited them out to gather at bachelors' quarters and bawdy houses. A few plied their businesses proximal to the ships' docks, greeting sailors who taunted chance, looking to the peril of their own woes.

The marked disproportion in males to females, the high tolerance for sport, and the appallingly lax regulation of liquor commerce conjoined to wreak disaster on many. It got so bad that it would be fair to say that first one purchased the bottle, rum preferred, and then he sought a reason for the celebratory occasion. As is usual when high levels of inebriation combine with liberated aggression, fistfights and felonious wounding were particularly remarkable for both their frequency and origin.

That scourge spared our family, particularly because Daddy was wiser. It wasn't that he abstained completely, but his consumption was rare, restrained, and downed at home. His yearly desire was a squat jug of imported Old Grog whiskey or the long-necked, green, opaque bottle of

Rotterdam Schiedam gin. His drinks lasted well into the New Year. He would make merry with a shot or two as friends customarily dropped in for the holidays. His aversion to rum shops matched his dislike for notorious houses of business and cook-shops. With the latter, one suspects that it was not merely sanitation that repulsed him. Well, let's look again at his roots and compare them with what was common at McKenzie from the fifties to early eighties.

Pre-research activities are necessary when looking for etiology of social problems. The activities help to inform the inquirer of what knowledge has already been documented and peer reviewed; what propositions others have made, their conclusions and so on. Collectively, literature on social problems suggest thus: if the phenomenon affects a few randomly dispersed persons, then there isn't a social problem. If the phenomenon is widespread and inimical to the community, then there is probably a social problem worthy of rigorous empirical research as to causation and possible amelioration.

While Daddy's attitude to alcohol taught us the benefits of moderation, some others in the community were not as measured and succumbed, as we shall see later. My mother's distant cousin Inez moved to Wismar with her husband. Tall, black, lithe, and comely, Inez was also soft-spoken and quiet by nature. One could not easily pair her with Thomas, her husband. She bore him four children, all clustered in ages. He worked for the company in a semi-skilled position. His pay compared favorably with other employees of that pay class. Thomas was a bit over six feet tall, stoutly built, and had a very wide girth. His voice had a deep resonance, which might have been admirable in an intelligent man. But Thomas, in company, usually appeared ill at ease and seldom had much to say even in casual conversion. His laugh, a belly-shaking guffaw could not ever be described as infectious. But he must have been attractive to Inez.

Problems plagued the family with swift viciousness. Inez complained to my mother about her husband's frequent drinking. Soon, it escalated to frequent drunken beatings. Because he was the sole breadwinner, she suffered the life-sapping role of the "good wife." Even the simple joy of anticipating payday was gone, as that was the day he would arrive home drunk, mean-spirited, and bellicose, with little or no money—all he'd earned gone to the liquor lords. Her mistreatment was heartbreaking. She soon joined the gaggle of mothers having similar problems, who waited at the company's front gate, hoping to intercept his paycheck before it could make it to the rum shop. Even that enraged Thomas. He beat her, knocked her teeth out, degraded her body and spirit to the point that she became a thin, sickly looking figure of her former zestful, admirable self. Rather than an occasional new dress, she wore her shame caused by the husband who had promised her love.

Their house had an unpainted bench; a bare, rough, wooden table; a few old beds; and plastic, upholstered chairs but not much else. Her kitchen utensils were old and battered. The flaked enamel told the truth of their poverty. As a young boy, I reached the bottom of myself with pity. Daddy and Mommy were there the Sunday we visited. They took the family home-cooked lunch and such. Thomas was there, ashamed, as could be determined by his bowed shoulders. My own impression was that he would have preferred to be elsewhere. The children played, laughed, and brought joy as only children can do, despite being dealt a bad hand. Yes, Thomas brought unnecessary suffering on himself and his family. This example of personal and parental failing is not unique. Nor is it the worst of possible heartbreak.

An interracial, childless couple living nearby struggled with alcohol addiction for all the many years of their marriage. The husband had occasional benders at the rum shops. Then in the evening, he would meander and stagger his way home. Sometimes unsure that he was at the correct intersection, he would stand for a minute or so, eyes fixed to the road, feet still, his body slowly twirling, in the fashion of a wobbly top, as his mind reeled in alcohol infused vertigo. It took much time, but eventually he would get home—after traveling both sides of the street and taking a few steps backward now and then as necessary for his stability. He was a quiet drunk and offensive to no one.

Unlike her husband's predictable inebriation, the wife's relationship with alcohol was that of an erratic binge drinker. Following a little over two months of near reclusiveness and sobriety, she would, shamefacedly, cross the street to a nearby house that surreptitiously sold liquor, and her determination overwhelmed by raging addiction, reluctantly purchases a large bottle of her preferred solace—rum. In the quiet of her dim home, she would sit all alone and drink herself to stupor. But the depth of her degradation had not yet been plumbed. About two days later, she would appear, knowing another battle has been lost—her steps smaller, slower, and more careful. This piteous, wrecked, wretched, woman would dejectedly cross the street once more, to replenish her blight from a woman of no conscience, a pitiless predator of the addicted. This vile, avaricious, mercantile creature was so greedy for a dollar, that she sold what was least needed to another human being who, at that point in time, had lost capacity to resist the drug and to care for herself.

With the mien of one condemned, shuffling, head low in despair, she would mechanically re-enter her home and lock the door. But this time, it would be different. Now all inhibitions had sunk in the depths of drunken abandonment. Unable to cook or feed herself, unable to leave her bed, her body would involuntarily relax the lower sphincter muscles. Her stomach's contents, nothing but alcohol sloshing about, her body soon rebels hurling its malodorous contents without caring where. When semi-conscious, whether day or night, at whatever hour, she would shout loudly her desire for libidinous satisfaction as salaciously as might be imagined. After a week of that, her own demons now themselves disgusted, she would return to normal consciousness, lonely and ashamed yet again.

Umpteen accounts tell of how alcohol ravaged the town, even though, for years, liquor licenses were not granted in McKenzie. Wismar and Christianburg were another matter. Magistrates granted license for the sale and consumption of alcohol but regulations pertaining to inspections and overall conduct of patrons and proprietors were seldom enforced. In fact, I know of no case taken before the court accusing a proprietor of any violation of a single regulation pertaining to the sale and consumption of spirits.

CHAPTER XIX

SECURING ONE'S OWN BONDAGE

DADDY LOVED SIMPLICITY of life, often extolling the avoidance of debt. Having had a rural upbringing and experienced the privations of the Great Depression and the war years, might have bent his traits at least toward cautiousness, if not frugality. This does not mean that he was contemptuous of debt of every kind. He was a member of the credit union, had a savings account there, and borrowed from the institution as necessary, where interest rate was fixed and lower. That is where he did business, not at the Portuguese-controlled branch of the Royal Bank of Canada, the only bank in town at that time. At that bank, all DEMBA paychecks were cashed at a window on a particular day of the week. At that bank one might see a very light complexioned, wavy-haired Black, but that was as diverse as the management allowed.

So, what was it about some credit transactions that he found contemptible? His distaste was reserved for those he deemed "land sharks." The most predacious of the lot was a man nicknamed Knocker, who had a business at Wismar. In the philosophy of some market-first types, Knocker might be exalted as enterprising, a self-made entrepreneur. But to Daddy, he was just another flea.

Knocker sustained himself by the control of men—those of weak spirit who surrendered their autonomy. These were the nightly revelers, the lazy, the base, the gluttonous, the shortsighted, the hapless, the desperate, and the complacently foolish. His was a business model, undifferentiated in nature to a cluster of intestinal parasites that will not be dislodged regardless of a medicine's vigorous scouring. As a service to the community, Knocker's kind is analogous to a disease that may or may not be fatal to the body. A parasite that has vital interests in the continued existence of the host but, even so, does nothing to aid its longevity.

At a cheap, shop-like hall with metal chairs and tables, Knocker provided lunch through dinner and more. The fare was mainly curried chicken, cook-up rice (a one-pot dish similar to paella) pepper pot, and a few choices of Chinese noodle meals. Patrons might sit and enjoy rhythm and blues, calypso, reggae, and such from a coin-fed jukebox while sipping alcoholic beverages. Female hang around would be there to comfort amorous men as their needs arose. Very soon, the pockets were empty, but further gratification need not be delayed; friend Knocker was always there to facilitate a usurious transaction. He would extend cash or credit, and like a leeching pawnbroker who thrives on the misery of others, Knocker demanded collateral and extortionate interest.

But be on guard against the likes of Knocker, do not be enticed or made a fool, the lender always secures collateral. If you have nothing fungible, he would settle for your very dignity. "Yes, of course," Knocker says amiably, as he accepts a valuable wristwatch that an impulsive buyer once thought needed; he'd take gold jewelry of any kind in lieu of cash. Not being too picky, Knocker would commit to "helping you out" by cashing your endorsed paychecks two days early. The fee for the transaction was 10 percent of the check's face value. Knocker was agreeable enough to continue to provide for his patrons' wants, even to the point of lending toward the anticipated checks. In other words, he would debit one's yet unearned income.

Daddy was critical of both victim and victimizer. A man who was master of himself distanced himself from that powerless behavior. As the Book of Proverbs counsels, "The borrower soon becomes the lender's slave."

In addition to the above, we ought to look closer at extravagancy, the cause of many of our intractable problems. It seizes us in ostentatious purchases and traps us in coarse, mind-numbing entertainment, but also, less recognizably, in habitual pursuit of the unnecessary. Think twice before spending money. If the purchase is not to fulfill an actual need, let the commodity be.

CHAPTER XX

THE DAY IT RAINED & DROWN THE PROFLIGATE

NO ONE NOTICED the smell of coming rain or the wind's shift. Too self-occupied with entertainment were they to have heard the barely audible, ominous rumble of the faraway thunder that preceded the figurative storm, soon to unleash economic and social havoc on the town. Fact is, had it been a thunderbolt, it would have been business uninterrupted. It is our nature to believe, despite all the human history of catastrophic occurrences, that tragedy strikes only other people, not us—other places, not here.

First came the sprinkle of soft rumors, but no reason, it seemed, for consternation. Faulty reasoning holds that, since no such calamitous occurrence was known to have befallen this economically sound company, there should to be no cause for alarm.

The whispered drizzle suggesting an oversupply of bauxite ore and the possibility of adverse consequences stayed within the engineering and supervisory class. It had a name no one wanted to hear—retrenchment! This was a name you quickly locked away at the back of the mind, since even its milder pseudonyms were fearsome. But soon it was all anxious people were talking about.

A few weeks later, the company formally announced that job cuts were impending and projected to be deeper than first thought. To ameliorate the impact, the company planned to create a "labor pool." Basically, that meant that the scores of workers in the pool would work in other departments in lower- paying positions. In the pool, one would lose about a third of one's accustomed earnings. The company promised that, as demand returned, it would reinstate the affected workers to positions commensurate with their previous positions. There was concern at all levels. But among the last hired, the low-skilled, and those without skills, the mood was somber, as they steeled themselves for the worst. It was now too late to start a savings plan. The pall was impossible to not notice. It wore on Daddy. I could tell by his slow pace, the sag of his shoulders as he rounded the corner home. He sat longer on the stoop of the front doorway, pensive, worried, head bowed and tilted. A few times, I heard him sharing his consternation with

Mommy. She was the more optimistic and applied herself to assuaging his fears as best she could.

It was an early evening on a weekday when Daddy called his family together. He sat on the second of three steps that led down to the kitchen. Mommy sat beside him. Cecil and I stood together. Dolly and Pinkey sat on the stairs with our parents. Dennis stood stoically to the right of the group, a little more distance than seemed appropriate. We all knew this was not good, as all was quiet and countenances glum. Mommy was looking down at her small hands folded on her lap, thinking and patient. Daddy told us about the pool and that the next day he would have to accept another job. He said it would be hard, and with reduced pay, he might have to withdraw Dennis and Cecil from high school. He had been paying school fees by weekly deductions. He was proud to have them in high school. Then he broke down and wept with deep sobs.

I began to cry. Cecil elbowed me in my left ribs. He scowled and mouthed admonishingly, "What you crying for?" I knew that Cecil had to maintain his tough facade. For him that was critical. Dolly cried. Pinkey cried. Dennis stood, his face inscrutable. Mommy said encouragingly, "Well, we'll have to make the best of it. Let's wait and see." I had no doubt that her mind was already working on combating what was to come. Giving in just was not natural to her.

The following day, Daddy went to work with the pool. I was in school and happened to look upon the main road, Arvida Road, which led to the bauxite treatment plant. Shock, shame, and fear melded to chasten me as I saw my father riding on a passing trash collection trailer pulled by a slow, small, red tractor. Two other men were back there with him. All sat precariously on the trailer's sideboard, arms outstretched sideways, holding on for balance. The minds of these three men, each somber-looking, were no doubt distant, weighing options to mitigate the pressing tribulation on their families. In the trailer, there were pitchforks and tree branches, which apparently, they had cleared. Daddy's head was bowed, his shoulders hunched. My father looked pitiable, and I was deeply sorrowed. Retrospectively, that might have shaped my understanding of life's randomness and my disposition to look out for and deal immediately with adversity every time it raises its despicable head.

There is use for everything that life springs upon us. Here was a man who did not scoff at catastrophe, who lived right, and yet he had been handed this trial. But he did not allow pride to cloud his judgment. He took what was available and, though disheartened, went immediately to work.

Later, at the end of the day shift, the second boot dropped hard. Hundreds received termination notices—with immediate effect noted. Some of the unfortunates had much more to worry about if they occupied low-rent company houses. In such cases, they had forty-eight hours to vacate the dwelling and McKenzie itself. The town being private property, they had no recourse under the Landlord and Tenant Protection Act. The tragic events brought the town as close as can be imagined to the Night of the Passover. It was wait and worry as the retrenchment took its toll.

This is the where you learn best from your parents' teachings and examples. From real-time experiences and how they dealt with them. It is also where you may learn by observing linkages between poor choices and consequences; that even with prudent decisions and careful living, crises do occur. Only some things are controllable; others are not. "That's life," Mommy says philosophically.

There was excitable sadness around the town. "Who's next?" "Did you hear?" Meanwhile, the suddenly destitute and desperate tried to dispossess themselves. A mass fire-sale ensued, all the more devastating since we had no prior experience of such a situation. The smoke stacks billowed 24-7 and 365, assuring a check would always be there, just like the water and electricity— self-deluded to smugness, we were.

Appliances, furniture, tools, jewelry—anything of value was sold at a fraction of its worth. Where there was a sale, both the seller and the buyer must have been ashamed to transact, the former knowing he was being taken but impotent of will and too choked by time to refuse, so dire his circumstances. The latter caught in ambivalence of wanting to help yet knowing deep within his duplicitous heart that he was taking advantage of the wretch's travail. The retrenched workers either returned to their coastal homes or removed themselves to nearby Wismar or Christianburg, hoping, waiting for a second chance. They had time to contemplate their situation and promise themselves that next time will be different.

About two days later, the sunshine returned to our lives. Daddy arrived home bubbling with confidence and exuberance. His perkiness made us all excited for his high spirits when he announced he had been removed from the pool and returned to his old job. For us, this was all a useful lesson well taught.

CHAPTER XXI

FILIAL DUTY HONORED AT ALL COST

IF ONE IS interested and knows what key behaviors to look for, it is possible to discover early a person's character by studiously observing how his or her time and money are spent. There are quite a few instances I could report on. But then this effort would be nothing better than a tabulation of good deeds and errors of a dutiful father or a chronicle of infectious diseases. So I'll restrict myself to examples.

During our time at McKenzie, many contagious diseases plagued the town, taking lives and leaving physical incapacitation in various degrees of severity. The victims were primarily children, the younger the more vulnerable. It did not help that we had an open sewer system, where the effluents were channeled by uncovered concrete gutters that paralleled each street and were discharged to three main trenches that, in turn, emptied into the Demerara River. Also dumped there eventually were some of the industrial wastes from bauxite treatment. Many people of Spightland, Wismar, and Christianburg bathed and did their laundry in the river. The first to attack was typhoid. That nearly succeeded in taking Cecil. The second, measles, nearly carried off Pinkey. Poliomyelitis was the most dreaded. Mommy's fear for her children was palpable. Pinkey's measles was pale compared to what Cecil suffered.

Typhoid struck Cecil when he was about five years old. Our parents visited him every day, though he was in the hospital's isolation ward. They took it hard, reporting that he could only wave bye-bye from behind a glass pane. Cecil was not responding to treatment as anticipated, his condition gradually moving to worse. The doctor was candid with my parents, informing them that the medicine being used had low efficacy. He presented an alternative treatment, which was prohibitively expensive. In fact, one dose was more than twice Daddy's earnings in a week. The amount was separate from the bill for hospitalization. That meant months of deductions from his paycheck.

Despite that, Daddy chose to take the option of the more aggressive, more expensive treatment. Cecil lost his hair but, after several weeks in hospital, he came home cured. Many other children, their parents unable to purchase that medicine, were not so fortunate. That was a concrete example of my father's virtuousness, he valued preservation of life above all material things. The choice he faced was not a simple one, considering he was the only breadwinner and had other children to provide for. (Pinkey was not yet born.) His decision showed selflessness and his exemplary character.

Dolly related another example of his loving tenderness. She explained that Dennis and she lived with our grandmother Adelaide during Mommy, Carmen, and Pinkey's sojourn in Barbados, where they stayed with Daddy's sister, Aunt Carlotta, for a few months. Daddy visited Dolly and Dennis every day, either on his lunch break or after work. One day, he saw that they were sick. Much displeased with their care, he set out for the pharmacy, where he bought medicines and then went home and cooked soup, which he brought for his children.

Dolly also recounted the day when two young children lost both of their parents on the same day. The father died in an industrial accident, and the mother died of a heart attack on receiving the news. Daddy went to their residence and brought the children to his home, where they were cared for a few days until their relatives were able to travel and get them.

Dolly also asked that it be noted that Daddy's blood type was rare, and he was called to the hospital occasionally to donate to the sick. He did not do it for any compensation. He just answered the call and gave.

Some may dispute with diminishing assertions that he did what any good father should for his children, especially Cecil during his sickness. To that I say, piffle! His compassion extended well beyond the sphere kinship bonds require, and he did for others without being asked. Documenting examples of his various selfless behaviors would be crass, lengthy, and maybe unpersuasive; that his deeds extended beyond the few examples I have given might best be left to the reader's intuition.

Daddy's father, James Henry King, died suddenly at his Canje home one midweek day. He was eighty-nine years old Louisa immediately informed Daddy of our loss and that the funeral was set for the following afternoon. The public announcement asserting that information would have already been made by the village bell ringer.

We knew something was amiss since Daddy arrived home about an hour earlier than normal and in haste. He told us of his father's demise and the funeral arrangements, explaining that he had taken the telegram to management and that they had secured for him a passage on an ore freighter, scheduled to leave in two hours or so, at the turn of the tide. Unfortunately, they said, he would have to travel on the open forward deck. In preparation for the cold night on the slow, ten-hour river trip to Georgetown, he carried a jacket folded across his arm. A change of clothing, funeral attire, toiletries, and such he gathered in a boxlike suitcase familiarly called a grip. Mommy, gave him something to eat on the way, her concern evident in the questions she asked of him. Assuring her he'd be okay, he gave her a peck, bade us all good- bye, and was off with alacrity. He had a little less than two miles to walk to the company's wharf.

Though it was some years since Canje was as previously described to be, the area remained undeveloped. Marginal improvement had been made, but it was still lacking much in domestic amenities and infrastructural conveniences. Death from natural causes, such as Mr. King's, was entirely a family affair, except for obtaining certification from his physician. Customarily, friends and neighbors gave support without being solicited. An all-night wake was quickly planned and attended. At such time, Louisa would have had the house lighted exceptionally bright with kerosene, gas-pressured lamps. Neighbors would have brought extra lamps. They would also have contributed plantains, cassava, crackers, coffee, and help preparing and serving modest snacks. No alcohol would have been present, though, since Louisa, a devout, abstinent Christian, forbade any imbibing. Windows and doors would have been open throughout the night. These would have been among Daddy's imaginings and expectations while on his long, heavyhearted journey.

I know that Daddy was quite aware that he was unwelcome aboard the vessel. That I discerned when Mommy asked about his travel accommodation. Surely, captain and crew of a large freighter with several decks of rooming could have afforded to, at the very least, be humane. The ship's crew offered him nothing, and Daddy asked for no more. Alone all night on the cold, forlorn, open forward deck of the ore freighter cloaked in the blackness of night broken only by the little luminance of navigational lamps, Daddy might have been reflecting on his father's life, his work, his maiming of his son, their remorse-laden relationship, forgiveness, and reconciliation. Surely, he would have preferred being at his father's wake singing "Abide with Me," "Amazing Grace," "How Great Thou Art" and reading aloud scriptural texts, Ecclesiastes 3 certain to be included. Such would have marked the gradual departure of the generation preceding his own—a final farewell to his father. Daddy's mournful tears would have freely flowed on the singing of his favorite, "O, Danny Boy," which I often heard him sing. They might have completed recitation and echo of John Ellerton's 1875 hymn:

> *Now the Laborer's work is o'er.*
> *Now the battle day is past; Now upon the farther shore Lands the voyager at last. Father, in Thy gracious keeping Leave me now Thy servant sleeping.*

There is good reason for the centuries-old traditions and ceremonies honoring the dead. Through them come the comfort of knowing that we are never alone. The heaviness of grief is a burden shared by all. We meet again long-lost relatives. Old friends come to remember, to share comfort, and to say good-bye. We have, together, one more chance to laugh, cry, and promise to stay in touch, another reminder of our temporality.

In provincial regions such as Canje, funerals must occur within forty-eight hours of death. Absent funeral homes and refrigeration, families similarly situated in tropical climes must act expeditiously in doing the necessities to retard the body's decomposition. Usually, the deceased is undressed and shrouded in a bed-sheet. The body is laid on a makeshift cold table, constructed of corrugated galvanized aluminum placed on wooden boxes or other means of elevation, waist high if possible. Blocks of ice, covered with sawdust to slow the ice's melting, follows that. Another aluminum sheet is set on the lot, and on this, the corpse is laid. Burlap sacks cover the body; smaller chunks of ice and sawdust are put on top, thus completing the process of slowing nature's urgent claim. Time is in the control of the dead. All must hurry to weep, say good-bye, consummate last rites and inter.

When Daddy returned home, we all gathered in the hall to hear of his trip and the sorrowful occasion—we, eager listeners, he, obliged to tell. He related that it was hard traveling all night on the ship's deck. "The cold," he said, "was almost unbearable." About seven o'clock the next morning the ship arrived at the estuary and anchored, awaiting a pilot to guide them safely beyond the dangerous sandbars to the open sea. The pilot arrived as passenger on a small launch, which, returning, ferried Daddy to Georgetown moorage. From there, he walked a short distance to the taxi park, where he hired a car to take him on the second leg of his journey, the sixty-mile drive to Rosignol. Daddy explained that he could not take the train or bus because he would have been delayed. His well-considered decision facilitated his arrival just in time for the graveside officiation. Daddy said that he and Louisa were his father's only kin in attendance. Others were neighbors or longtime friends. I could not detect exactly how this significant episode of his life affected him emotionally, but since he was the only son and needing so much to unburden his father's guilt, it must have been especially anguishing.

This particular event was of profound importance. Later I realized that my father was so committed to filial principles that no one could have dissuaded him from undertaking such fatigue, such distant, time-bound, primitive travel to witness his father's burial and say final farewell. The 130-mile overnight, multiple mode travel was demanded of him by none but loyalty. After all, he regularly wrote his father endearing letters, visited, and sent money as far back as memory serves me. So there really was nothing he had to make up for. Some might have different expectations of paying respect. For some, it might have been just as well accomplished by a later visit to the grave, offering prayers and laying a wreath. Another option may have been to pen a letter of shared grief to console Louisa. Yes, there were alternatives. There are always alternatives. But in my father's moral world, those options were anathema. So ingrained were his values, this last obligation, I believe, would have been served even if Daddy had to walk the distance to meet the enduring, venerate duty of the child to the departing parent. That is a moral command so imperative few would not honor.

His father bequeathed him a plot of land (an acre or so), the house, and a gold ring. It was large, weighty, plain, and roughly crafted. In fact, it was a crude piece of worn, scratched jewelry questionable in karat. Its value was, without doubt, principally nostalgic. Along with that, Daddy brought home his father's huge Bible. It was recognizably ancient, heavy, and almost a foot thick. When together, the leaves appeared to be varnished gold, glossy at the three edges. The thin pages needed careful handling. It seemed little used, a conclusion drawn from the fact that there were no dog-eared pages, smudges, or any sign or steady use. His Bible bore exquisitely decorative lettering and colorful pictures of saintly ascetic men graced with halos, mostly. Serene women and children populating the holy book were fewer but there, nevertheless. The Bible's dark brown, hefty covers bore a stout cross, carved-looking, and embossed, the whole constructed to tolerate a lifetime of sound thumping.

He brought his father's bicycle also. It was of another age, it seemed. Long and heavy-framed, it boasted a conspicuous saddle made of hard leather and a curiously curved spring support that spiraled and jutted upward.

Zealously he approached the work of refurbishing his father's bicycle, but since he was able to buy a new one, it might have stirred much curiosity as to why he took on the extraordinary work and expense to make the old new again. However, it was purposeful.

The derelict wheels were oversize, they needed custom fitting for tires and inner tubes. Daddy spent hours restoring the bicycle, and later he proudly rode it to work. It was the manifestation of his emotional connection to his father.

This inherited assortment of corroded metal and dry-rotted rubber might, to the disinterested, be an unexplainable waste of time—even kooky. For Daddy, however, this was the resurrected personification of the ideal father he never had and the dutiful son he longed to be. The bicycle's tangibility offered another chance to peddle back in time, to fix all that was so broken or ignored, undoing the wrongs, promising to be caring and lovingly attentive in reminiscences and memorials. Thus, for a couple of weeks, he vigorously abraded neglected spokes, rims, chain, and sprockets. The rims he painted silver; scrubbed, moistened, and polished the leather saddle. For refitting tires, cogs, and such he contracted the services of Mr. Cummings, who owned the local cycle repair and rental shop.

Despite all the time and effort both men spent, they could not get the brake levers to work as designed.

Replacements were no longer produced. At tryouts, the bicycle slowed for want of peddling; he would pull the lever repeatedly, hoping for the needed result. Sometimes, he misjudged his speed and could not stop where he wanted. But he improvised with due emergency measures. That is to say, he used his feet, causing the bicycle to wobble. It was so funny to see his concentrated efforts, him dragging his boots on the unpaved road to stop where he wished. Invariably, he arrived in a cloud of reddish dust. But he was satisfied, perhaps thrilled. This went on until one day he was stopped by a bored policeman and cited.

Work done. Time and money unstintingly spent, soon came the day he joyfully mounted the heirloom and proudly took his father's place on the saddle. From time to time, people asked him about his strange, antiquated bicycle, such a "conversation piece" it was. On those welcomed occasions he perked and told tales of his father and his bicycle.

CHAPTER XXII

BEHIND EVERY SUCCESSFUL WOMAN

NO ONE WOULD have thought of my parents being a likely couple, so different were they in many ways. She was shorter than the average woman, standing only about five-foot four at best, but in her high-heeled shoes she was quite noticeable. Her walking beside Daddy emphasized their physical differences in height, body type, and complexion. They also comported themselves differently. She stood erect, her head held high, and was usually carefully dressed to the occasion. In an encounter with others, she was most likely to speak before him and persist further than an initial no. Should he be the first to speak, be assured she would not stand silent. She would ensure that she understood the discussion and any decisions or commitments derived therefrom. One such occasion involved a teacher, Mr. Blount, a young man who subordinated his role as teacher and assumed the position of class bully. Kids dreaded his class. One day, he got overexcited and went about the class hurrying us, randomly hitting whomever he pleased. Mr. Blount slapped my head. A prescient onlooker might likely have exclaimed, "Oh, big mistake! Now look at what yo' gone and do." I told my mother what had occurred. The following morning, on his walk to school, she clapped and having got his attention, asked him to wait. She went onto the street and spoke with him. It was a short conversation. I do not know what she told him, but whatever it was, he instantly understood her expectation. From that day Mr. Blount mended his ways. He never again abused his position.

Nearly ten years separated our parents in age, but one would not notice that at a cursory glance. They had just about the same level of education, yet Mommy seemed the more dominant during discourse, even just between them. It was quite funny to hear them talk about traversing Georgetown or New Amsterdam. The minutia! They seemed joined in a harmless contest as to which knew the cities best. That's where their similarities in attitudes and personality were most noticeable.

My parents rose from humble beginnings. Both bore the burden of being unwanted children. In those days, the well-intentioned but stigmatizing English Bastardy Act was in full ruinous effect. Mommy was handed off to her great-aunt, who raised her well, was reportedly obsessively strict but not abusive. All she knew of her father was his last name. He never supported her and never visited or communicated with her. She had not even seen a photograph of him.

As a couple my parents were a well-respected, dynamic team. The social elevation they attained while raising six children far beyond their own life chances, would astound theorists of determinism. Mommy was as indefatigable as Daddy was resolute. Earlier, I related their industry in creating additional income by catering snacks to construction workers and Daddy moonlighting as a plumber at houses some weekends. It would be a reasonable conjecture that the idea for the former was hers. However, it was all hands in once the catering business was started. When the buildings were complete and the workers left, our cottage business ceased. Mommy did not waste time moving on to something else. She always had an eye for enterprise and opportunity.

I could cite numerous examples of my parents' success through working in consort to the benefit of all of their children, themselves, and their relatives. Mommy identified the path to perceived opportunities, and Daddy executed—that was their simple formula for success.

It was while in Barbados that Carmen met and married Clifton Neblett, and they all returned to British Guiana. The couple lived briefly with our grandmother Adelaide, then came to live with us. My parents discussed speaking with the school principal, and Daddy wasted no time on that. Clifton, being qualified and working towards his degree in accounting, was hired as a teacher within a week. The kids loved him. His peculiar accent amused them, but much more important, I think, Clifton was an affable person. The kids tended to gravitate to him and called him affectionately, Mr. Nebbie. He soon found a much better paying job with the bauxite company and, having saved enough, the young couple set their sights on England, where Clifton qualified as a certified accountant and Carmen as a certified nurse. They accomplished all this within the space of a few years.

At the risk of being in sequential, I must talk about their ambition. Clifton and Carmen had the option of living in McKenzie, where they would have had a safe, comfortable, but mundane existence. Or migrate to England for more challenging, interesting lives. They wisely chose the latter. Our parents convened a farewell party for them. No dancing, just a two-hour occasion to chat, take photographs, and share some wine and company. When, after short prayers, it came time to toast the couple, the well-wishers seemed to be vying for a rich prize as to which was most able to scare the bejesus out of the couple. Among tears, gifts, and exhortations to be good ambassadors for our country, they spoke of the daring journey by sea to an unknown situation and warnings of the pitfalls to avoid. Really, I should not have been surprised if the couple had considered not leaving at all, after such a well-meaning attack on their temerity. But the guests intended no discouragement and were merely following custom.

When Clifton and Carmen came to live with us, there were then nine of us living in the small house already described, but we managed. Mommy would always say, optimistically, "we'll make the best of it". My brothers and I shared a bed placed in the kitchen. Our parents got rid of the indestructible, commodious wood-burning stove and replaced it with a modest kerosene range. They bought a double bunk bed and did whatever was possible and necessary to make us all comfortable yet be hospitable to cousins visits. We never turned our backs on kin.

The end of the school year came around. Children were out of school for two months. Daddy, spoke with a couple living nearby about a temporary office job for Cecil. They were close to the management staff and friendly toward us. Within a few days, Cecil got a job at the personnel office. More income came to the family. Cecil netted both work experience and confidence.

The next year, at her own expense, Mommy managed to send Dennis and Cecil on a touring camp to the island Trinidad. Traveling by ship, my brothers spent two weeks there, played scheduled cricket matches, and generally enjoyed their vacation. Imagine their excitement. What that opportunity must have been like for young teens. It no doubt boosted their self-assuredness, raised their expectations of themselves, and expanded their horizons beyond a parochial neighborhood.

With influence of a family friend and letters of recommendation secured from persons of prominence, including Rev. Father Hale, my parents helped Dennis get a job at Radio Demerara, where he learned the technical skills of audio engineering. That opportunity was the foundation on which Dennis built and achieved incredible success and international recognition in the music recording industry. Employed by Atlantic Records in New York, he would later boost the performance and popularity of several artists and rhythm and blues groups. Armed with a strong work ethic and a character suited to the work, my brother built on the initial support of his parents. Dennis was able to create a wonderful life for himself, his equally persevering wife June, and their children. No easy accomplishment in the United States.

That same year my parents helped Cecil with his office job, they turned their attentions on me. With school out for the July- August end of term, Mommy suggested to Daddy that he should consider speaking with Mr. Mitchell about a temporary job for me at the post office. "After all," she said, "Leyland will be out of school for two months with nothing to do." He thought only briefly, got up and hurried off to the post office. His speed was due in part to the post office's scheduled closing at noon on Saturdays.

Upon his return, he informed that Mr. Mitchell had promised to "put in a word" for me with the postmaster Mitchell, the senior postal clerk, was a short, affable fellow on assignment from another district on the coast. He had become known to us through his wife, a regular patron of my mother's beauty parlor. She had once hosted us at their home for a Sunday visit. Mr. Mitchell was one of those few people you couldn't imagine bearing malice toward another. His broad, genuine smile overcame any such thought.

One morning, about two days after Daddy had spoken with Mr. Mitchell, the postmaster sent word that I should appear for an interview. Mommy was all excited about the call. Fussy about how I should dress, she ensured that nothing denied me the opportunity. I wore my best and made anxious haste to the post office not far away. Meeting with the PM was no trivial thing, we thought. (It was customary to refer to the person of that position as PM. Sometimes the surname followed, but more often, it didn't.) Mr. Mitchell greeted me at the side door. His smile attested his pleasure. We shook hands briskly. The clerks swung to take notice. Mr. Mitchell walked me over to meet the postmaster. Unlike the beaming Mr. Mitchell, the PM greeted me with cool politeness. Behind round, thick-lensed spectacles, his weary, hooded lids whispered "patience." He seemed tired and bore the resignation of one who had long since concluded that there was, indeed, nothing new under the sun. We appraised each other, him with a speculative air. He soon appeared to be satisfied with his observations.

Retrospectively, I saw in him a quiet man. He was a clean, decent gentleman, who did not manage to continue living vitally in his own time. The postmaster was, I believe, unable, unwilling, or maybe uninterested in keeping abreast of the changes that spring upon one who believes he is incapable of lifelong learning. He was a man who probably regretted staying too long on a single career, his only occupation in his whole life. With upward mobility based on seniority, he'd have found chances narrowing as he ascended. He would patiently wait on his yearly increment, which all got regardless of their contribution -how hard one worked, or carefully shirked. He respected the values— obedience, forbearance and avoidance. Now he possessed no needed skills and discovered belatedly that he had no prospect of further promotion. For him, each day had become a more inopportune time to leave. With a large steel and concrete safe about six feet from his desk, the sum of his physical exertion at work peaked at the single-digit steps from his desk to the usually wide open safe. Currently, bound against his true will, laden with bunches of jingling, mostly useless, tarnished keys, he was destined to count, add, and subtract in the government's heaven's gate ledger until pension eligible retirement, all the while bitterly cognizant that even Sisyphus wouldn't consider swapping repetitious jobs with him.

Mr. Mitchell stood by the postmaster's desk, then said, "This is the young man we talked about, sir."

We shook hands, PM and I. "Oh yes, yes," PM agreed, adding, "My, you are a tall one." His comment was casual, emphasizing the verb.

They all laughed. I smiled, relieved. PM leaned back all the way in his wooden swivel chair, which, along with a broad, sturdy desk, were elevated on a platform in the middle of the office. The old chair creaked again on its way forward. In the dim light of the post office, the PM looked at me paternally as he wiped his brown-rimmed glasses with a handkerchief and then queried unexpectedly, "When can you start?"

"Um, now?" I said, and they both laughed again.

It was left to Mr. Mitchell to inform me about hours, pay, and other consequential things.

The job was supposed to be casual, for the holidays. I ended up working there for the next three years. I started delivering telegrams and then the first of three mail routes; a counter position followed, all for the same pay as the day I'd started.

Mommy was exceedingly proud. Daddy went along but didn't express much. Again, employment they'd arranged meant more income for the family, excellent work experience, and confidence for their son.

What is rudimentarily portrayed here is the way loyalty and influence work, at any level, in any group, at any place and time, to varying degrees. Meritocracy is a great and wonderful ideal, a useful principle, but the world does not work that way. It never has and probably never will. Had that not been the case, the world's gentry would have been less inbred, and little princes would sweat for their bread. Had that not been the case, oligarchy's insidiousness could not root and nincompoops would not even be suffered to live. It is the leveraging of opportunities that makes our worlds turn. The more traditional the society, the greater the reliance on the strength of blood ties, social kin, clans, guilds, and lodges. There are also gentlemen's private clubs; college fraternities and their inner, secret cliques; and the powerful unity of faith. Closer to the core of wealth and privilege, we have trusts, chambers of commerce, lobbyist, and socialites all facilitating the influential handshake.

Few are they who improve their lives unaided in some small, seemingly insignificant way. In fact, I would be hard-pressed to think of anyone who did not so benefit by another's felicity. The exception is, of course, the fictional hero, Howard Roark, of The Fountainhead (1943), a popular, inauthentic novel written by soi-disant philosopher and writer Ayn Rand and adapted to the screen. There are at least a dozen men and women, unrelated to me, who just happened to be at the right time, the right place, with the right actions, power, or counsel to whom I shall always be grateful. In fact, I might say that, but for them, my wise, farsighted benefactors, life might have been quite different for me and, perhaps, for those to whom I, in turn, was able to provide fellowship and guidance. Once, it was just encouragement when my spirit flagged. Another helped me navigate life's treacherous shoals by providing timely intelligence. Another "put in a word," and yet another just unlocked the door, without my solicitation and moved on. But this is what's strange about life—I never asked any of those particular persons for help. Yes, they provided me aid all unsolicited, expecting nothing in return.

But then there are lesser others who, upon seeing you, or otherwise being alerted to your coming and goals, begin fervidly nailing the door shut. Could they make it so, the door would be hermetically sealed. This goes on more frequently, yet we live in a culture that pretends the contrary to be true. So we obstruct, we deny, and we forget. We play mind games. We practice deceit.

But that does not in the slightest obviate your responsibility to yourself and kin. It does not undo call to work harder, struggle indomitably, sacrifice ascetically, burn the midnight oil, and go the extra mile, applying yourself to broad education and skill proficiency as complex as you are able. Another's benevolence cannot "hook you up" or "grease the hinges" for you to be hired as a scientist, doctor of medicine, or an attorney of substance. But once you are duly qualified, he or she can facilitate your professional ascension by influencing where you intern, where you clerk, who mentors you, and the associations best suited to your aspirations. Simplified, a benefactor can only groom what is potentially there. Don't be arrogant and, moreover, don't be ill advised. Ah, just say it. Don't be stupid! Pull on your own bootstraps "till Kingdom mornin' come." You'll be right where you are with only a painful, curved spine and frayed straps to show for your efforts. Looking downward, your attention captured by your bootstraps means you cannot see opportunity's star. Obsessed with looking downward, you'll soon eat bitterly off the ground.

I am grateful to Mommy, then de facto head of our family, who understood this intuitively and employed leverage to push her own children first. Show me a social, religious, racial, ethnic, class or group that does not utilize personal connections, influence, and leveraging—that believes in luck and other magical thinking—and I'll show you a group perennially penurious, marginalized, and mendicant.

CHAPTER XXIII

WHAT DID WE BELIEVE

WE BECAME CATHOLIC for the singular, mundane reason that the Roman Catholic Church, dedicated to Saint Joseph the Worker, was situated about two hundred yards northwest of our house. But for a right turn onto Arvida Road, the partial obscurity by Nurse Johnson's residence, and a long bachelors' quarters, I would have been able to say that the church was within sight, and, on a quiet night, a good hailing would get one's attention.

We might have been affiliates of the Church of England's Christ the King had the building not been located a little farther and in the opposite direction on the same Arvida Road. To that one, Christ the King, our grandmother devoted membership. It happened to be so much nearer to her house on Crabwood Street. Both houses of worship were about the same size and architectural design—wide entrances on three sides and fine, thick hardwood doors so colossal they demanded much energy of an altar boy to swing them shut on the rare occasions they were shut. The embellishments, big, bronze hinges, brass knockers, and oversize framework added their bit to the weight but also aided the impression of permanence, durability, and reverend awesomeness. The doors of each edifice were stained brown and polished but not with a sheen. I suppose that was deliberate craftsmanship, owing to the fact that, even the untrained eye, could not miss nature's unique designs in the timbers' course grain. The churches were both painted the identical shade of eggshell white. Both were secluded in the way places of worship everywhere simultaneously welcome and intimidate the beholder. Both churches boasted wide concrete perimeter promenades, over which the roofs generously sloped, providing shade convenient for the priests' pacing back and forth, sometimes circumventing the building, during their scheduled solitary prayers. Neither building had windows, and no stained glass graced either. But the lofty ceilings and large doorways militated against heat accumulation. These houses of worship were positioned close to the riverbank. The black, slothful river added expanse to the vistas; soft, moderating breezes; and, perhaps, serenity to some souls. But it's merely speculative whether that was in the planners' creative imaginings. Their placement seemed to be of more immediate, practical considerations. The plain wood plank landings behind each church were there I deduced, to facilitate funeral obligations and convenience for those residents from across the river who wished to attend services say funeral concerns because of the fact that it was common at thnerivoetrh.er in English, the beliefs represented were really of no doctrinal importance to us. It was said to be good to go to church.

Therefore, we went to church. Yes, it was as conforming as that the time to bear the decreased by boat to the cemetery a few miles downriver.

The clergy, Father Hale, and Father Brown and later, Father Pink were all White, friendly expatriates from Britain. The last a pugilist years earlier was robust and energetic of disposition. They lived sparingly in similar houses on the churches properties.

Save for the fact that one priest conducted Mass in Latin and miles downriver.

On Mondays, our school had only to get together two columns of students, one to each denomination.

We thus proceeded three abreast, chaperoned by a few teachers, for religious teaching. If you were Hindu,

Muslim, or of any other religious belief, you could attend church or remain at school. The battle for the course of the mind begins early. Most of us traverse life believing what our parents and their parents held to be true. We hold these beliefs so passionately that death be welcomed or imposed rather than we deviate from one tittle of religious stipulation. For us, it was merely which church was closest to our house. Had Jehovah's Witnesses or the religious body been there, we would have been avid, pious adherents of one of those creeds. That simple it was. Why think for yourself? It may lead to unbearable cognitive dissonance. Why frighten yourself? That may lead to existential anguish and dispositional unease.

I do not know of anytime our parents went to church, but they must have had occasion to visit, since we were all baptized Catholics. Pinkey remembers Daddy taking the three of us, Dolly, her and me, to Mass one Christmas Day. That might well be true, but I do not recall it. So what did we believe? To answer sincerely, though we were all baptized Catholics, we may still accommodate elements of competing faiths and practices, assimilating, discharging and expanding continually as doctrines evolve. One may order what is important to him or her, but in the face of severe, prolonged hardship or peril, we tend to revert to our fundamental cultural traditions for deliverance. A little extra indemnity for the after-life harms no one. For evidence, consider the vitality of Christianity, Judaism, Muslim, and other faiths that have survived hundreds of years of horrid, relentless persecution. No different from any other is the longevity of African beliefs, religious customs, and folklore. Dismissed by colonial thinking as mumbo jumbo for reasons that are obvious. Before discussing my parents' beliefs, we ought to give some attention to European superstitions—just a bit, a teeny bit.

It was at the movies that I first heard the words mumbo jumbo— particularly applied to African religious beliefs, their languages, or their broader cultural contexts. The intentions of those who used the label are clear. But what is interesting is that the label is never applied to Euro-Christian institutions. Despite all the visible evidence, we never see European superstitions there gargoyles on some buildings in the most advanced societies but a totem pole is regarded as meaningless, grotesque art? What is it about the number thirteen? Or triple six for that matter? Are there not scores of superstitions among seafarers, athletes, and gamblers? Why would a country elect someone to the highest office, knowing full well that his decisions might be influenced by his faithfulness to astrological readings of the day, tarot cards and numerology? The answer is very simple, it's because superstition is normal, though illogical.

European Dracula got his dinner just like the Ol' Higue of British Guiana did. The differences are that she never proceeded to seduce her victims during the bloody feast. Nor did she demand eternal loyalty in master-servant relationships. Whereas garlic was Dracula's repellant, salt was the Ol' Higue's bane. Much cheaper. If trapped, he gets a stake in the heart, while she is metaphysically bound counting grains of rice and cannot get back into her salted skin. At any rate, they do have commonality in the imperative to get home by their unpardonable curfew time—dawn. Whereas he flaps clumsily home puffing as any gorged, bloated bat would, she rockets home a fireball in the sky. He should beware collision. They, like some politicians, cannot survive sunlight. We could go on, but that would be too digressive.

Now we can at least agree with a proposition that, maybe, humans are mostly irrational and superstitious. Daddy was in and out of hospital, though never known to be sickly. He would go to bed, and in the wee hours, a violent, uncontrollable, shaking of his body would occur. Mommy, alarmed on the first instance called upon the ambulance service. At the hospital, the physician diagnosed ague fever (malaria). Daddy was hospitalized for about a week each time. My mother's suspicion grew around what exactly was causing his illness.

It was a little after the vesperal bell rang, when it is said to have manifested. Daddy was in his accustomed position at the uppermost step of the front stairway, reading his newspaper in the twilight. I saw Sister Stella, Dolly's godmother, walk through her backyard, cross the red loam road, and ascend the stairs, whereupon she asked Daddy to get up and go into the house with her, which, seeming puzzled, he did. She reported that she saw a figure of a tall man standing over Daddy. Sister Stella knew what she saw.

Mommy got busy. She went to Father Hale, who provided, among other items, a blessed amulet. I don't know what more she did, but whatever the reason, the sighting never happened again. And co-incidentally, Daddy was never again hospitalized for that malady. Before a good guess be formed, remember that malaria may reinfect the host a few times before the disease is removed completely from the body. What to believe is entirely up to the reader.

So, to return to what my parents' believed. Demonstrably, they were Christian leaning, but practice of faith was not included for themselves. It might be best to say that they respected religion, but commitment and participation just weren't there.

CHAPTER XXIV

IT MAY BE MUCH DARKER THAN IT SEEMS

SOMETHING INDEFINABLY ODD was occurring in our home that night. My sisters were speaking animatedly but in tones in the kitchen, but I was uninterested in what might have been the hush's cause. When they did come to me, I deployed my strategic interaction dissuader— I pretended not to notice. Then they called me with a little more anxiousness of tone. My distinct sigh of exasperation was insufficient to faze my two determined sisters. Yes, it was Dolly and Pinkey again! They just would not let me read in peace. Harpies both! It looked like I would have to give them my devastating scowl, a second level of my defenses that had proven very effective in the past.

"Leyland! Leyland, Mommy going to kill herself," said they with subdued excitement and trepidatious concern. I was skeptical.

"Man, yo' all always with something. Why would she kill herself?" I questioned rhetorically, throwing in a dismissive frown.

They scampered off, first Dolly with Pinkey close behind. Delighted to see that the tactical facial expression had retained its potency, I settled more comfortably into the soft-textured, colorful upholstery of the wooden Berbice chair that occupied much of the living room. Now I had the chair and a great book all to myself. Nirvana!

Pleased that my studied, commonsense response was effective, I returned to my book, but with waned enthusiasm and unsettling thoughts.

Could it be true? I second-guessed my initial dismissal of my sisters' supposition.

Of course not. Mommy seemed quite normal to me some hours ago, I reasoned.

But the seeds of disquiet, sown in my mind, had begun sprouting. They nettled and pricked at my short-lived pod of serenity.

What if it is true though? I pressed myself. Then came conscience's accusatory, finger pointing at me. You were warned, its owner said. You could have stopped it. You killed her!

I got up and set aside my book without a bookmark. Immediately, the terrible two came again babbling in unison.

"Leyland, I think she's going to kill herself in truth," Dolly said, sounding frightened. "She kissed Pinkey and told her good-bye." "Yeah?!" I said, now taking them very seriously indeed. "Where is she?"

"She's going through the shortcut, by Miss Henley's.

"Come, come," they urged. "Let's see where she's going," Pinkey added.

Knowing that Mommy and Miss Henley were friends, I said, "Well, she might just be going to visit Miss Henley."

As I rationalized, the three of us stood in the backyard; the girls were getting more agitated. Eyes wide, both of them were suggesting what should be done next. We agreed that we must follow her. First though, we had to see her, which meant we had some catching up to do. The three of us started running through the backyard, crossed Greenheart Street, and continued our pursuit.

This was well after nine o'clock, and we were on the sprint through several dark backyards. I knew the way well and knew also which houses had "bad" dogs; which had ricies -timid yappers with no bite; and, most of all, which had hazardous clotheslines of strung wire that could grab a reckless neck and, before a runner knew what had happened, lay him flat on his back coughing painfully.

We weren't able to see her, for the dark. The sisters were now ceaselessly expressing their troubles, while I endeavored to discount what was becoming more dreadfully evident and urgent. We were worried for our mother because the route she was taking was so desolate. I seldom walked that route at that time of night. After all, it was near the northern end of the Catholic Church, and the jamoon trees' low-hanging branches created foreboding shadows to the dismay of the superstitious, the timorous, and those of loose imagination. A few yards farther, was the Portuguese lady's grave. She disliked having her daisies' petals plucked and was reputed to be quite frightening, according to children's after- church tales. The aluminum painted, wrought iron enclosure could be eerie at night. Here was a single unnamed resting place from long, long ago.

"Let's check by the boat landing," one of my sisters suggested. "Yes, she might be going to the river there."

My sisters, out of breath but persevering, were talking concurrently, and my attention seemed to be straying. I really couldn't tell who had made the suggestion and who had agreed. At this time we were running, and I was sometimes walking briskly, so that my sisters could keep up. We were now approaching the boat landing's sandy footpath, which led from the road to the river—the same pedestrian-worn track where, a few years past, Cousin Brandis, with a cutlass, had decapitated his wife in a single swipe. Such dark, heavy shadows, and not a soul in sight. We kept up the pursuit.

"Look, look, I see her. She's going to the river!" Dolly exclaimed and repeated herself. Then, having realized that her fears were fast becoming reality, she cried louder in earnest repetition, "She going to the river!"

"Where? Where?" I asked.

Dolly pointed. It was then that I saw Mommy's unmistakable silhouette. She was walking calmly toward the river, all alone on that dismal, narrow trail. She was only about thirty yards or so from the bank of the pitch-black, unforgiving Demerara River, and not a ferryboat nor even another person was in sight. A dim, short, wicked kerosene lamp hung lopsided on what may best be portrayed as something between a stick and a short pole to guide the ferry. The flickering lamp light, made dim by sooth, served less to luminesce, and offer some feeling of safety than to accentuate the creepy isolation of the boat-landing and the surrounding gloom.

"Leyland, you go ahead. You can get to her first. Oh, God!" the girls urged.

I broke off from them and ran swiftly the length of the trail. And when I'd caught up with our mother, I hugged her and wept. She wore her brown, woolen, light sweater and dark dress. With my arms around her, I realized how small she was, how distressed and vulnerable she appeared. Strangely, she had been unconcerned about the sound of running feet behind her in so bleak a place. She either did not hear or did not care, so disconnected from herself she had become.

Dolly and Pinkey arrived on the run. Between gasps, someone asked her why she was "doing this."

She replied in a strange, affectless way, "Why not? You see how he's treating me."

I was shocked at her tearless nonchalance. My mother had in fact already resigned from life itself.

Now it was all three of us "hugging on her," crying, and telling her we loved her and would protect her. And who would take care of us when she wasn't there?

Turned around, we walked her home with slow steps and no further talk. She didn't cry. Her countenance was flat, her eyes, disinterested. This was a person who had had enough. With tearful sniffs and sniffles, we together made our way home at her pace, but I was angry. I had seen him hit her before, just because she'd told him, quite calmly, that he'd wronged a neighbor. For Daddy and me, our ships were abreast. But the courses would intersect if this continued. Come to think of it, we had never talked about the occurrence, even among the four of us involved, and I won't be surprised if some members of the family are unaware of it. When we got home, we entered by way of the still open kitchen door. All was quiet but not owing to the late hour. Daddy was still up. He sat alone toward the front of the house, looking out the window, no doubt bitterly ruminating. He probably did not even know that we had left the house. Dolly and Pinkey remained with Mommy in the kitchen. The home was quiet, though by no means calm. It was still with a tension one sensed. I approached my father and politely informed him of the near tragic incident at the riverside.

What my expectation was I did not know. Thus, I was unprepared for the unfeeling retort. He did not get up. My father just turned his head; looked at me briefly; and spoke the most shocking, apathetic words—grievously appalling to the situation at hand. "Well," he said dismissively, "why did you stop her?" He then resumed his simmering.

I turned and quietly walked back to the kitchen. I did not want to see or talk to anyone. I did not wish to be angry at anyone. I suspect that, by then, my emotions had long gone to a safer place. The tragedy had been averted; now I wanted to let it be. Just let it be!

Humility knows that some things cannot be explained. It accepts that no one may presume to know the heart of another, that the last step determines the next, and that not all things are within our control. I can only wonder what could have made my mother so forsaken of spirit and my father as frigid as a winter's rock. His bitterness and her resentment had reached unfathomable depths. This marriage was now the very definition of "irretrievably broken."

CHAPTER XXV

REVELING IN ANOTHER'S TROUBLE

TROUBLE, ONCE ARRIVED, must be collared at the doorstep, and there a fierce, unrelenting butt kicking be inflicted. Trouble must know that you are in charge and uncompromising. Allow no entreaties and cajoling! His intent is to enter your home, unpack, and begin consuming the tranquility within. Since trouble adores company, he calls over his ugly, rambunctious, mischief-making cohorts, who thrive on strife. Peace, fed up with the prevailing situation, judiciously takes speedy flight.

When air travel became possible, the record of fatal accidents was not reassuring to any commuter. Humankind, curious as we are, subjected every failure to rigorous analysis. Laboratories studied simulated models. All focused on answering these questions: What caused the failure and how do we prevent its recurrence? Resultant was the constant improvement of air transport. The analogy to marriage and family relationships, admittedly a bit loose fitting, cannot be precisely applied because of the inability of predicting and controlling for human emotions and rationality. Nevertheless, behaviors and statements may lead reasonable persons to infer and imply that the congregation of information points to theories of what might have happened to precipitate the so-called "failure" of our parents' marriage. I would like to know what might have contributed to the dissolution. It is important for me to know, if only for the sake of knowing. But it is also quite possible that each of them might have had very different reasons for the breakup, some known or unknown to one or both. That being so, I caution against firm presumptions. But we may get to better understanding even if we meander a bit to arrive there.

Earlier I commented on our sibling grouping. Three children before the departed Kenrick, and three after. That was how we bonded. Our first group, Carmen, Dennis, and Cecil, left home in an orderly, supportive manner. It was quite different for the second three. A clue may be drawn from Mommy's comment at the point of her decision to leave. "Everybody's grown up now and can take care of themselves," she said.

It was a strange expression, but set it against the fact that, up to the day of her statement, her life had been toil, toil, and more toil. She was mother, wife, homemaker, hairstylist, doctor in residence, finance manager and counselor, among umpteen other roles. Her reflection of her life may have revealed it to her as a trial of overwork. Perhaps there is more to consider. A cursory literature review on the subject explains that marriages have cycles, and similar to the organic world, family relationships and composition are in continuous states of change. Each and all growing, possibly atrophying, at different rates. Stasis cannot be. As in the well-known metamorphosis of chrysalis to butterfly, the family as a unit is subject to gradual processes of transformation, from conception to expiration.

To tease out the cause of the end of my parents' marriage, we would want to know what their premarital relationship was like. Knowing that Daddy was nine years her senior and, at that time, a low wage earner with little prospect for improvement, we might wonder if there were any apprehensions. The officiation of the marriage marked the first stage, that is, life together as a couple. How did the relationship change following the birth of their first child? How did it change again on the arrival of the second and so on? Other changes may have been centered on income. Remember my father was then a laborer, and his pay was irregular.

It is reported that traditional marriages such as my parents' quake under the pressures of the wife becoming an independent wage earner. The fact that her income often exceeded his could not have helped, in terms of new realities in chores, decision- making, and intimacy. But nothing that we children had become aware of even hinted at that being a problem. Daddy was always supportive of Mommy's ambitions, often materially too. Then again, how would I know?

Mommy took "the course." That was what everyone used to refer to the training of a hairstylist and beautician. She did very well, graduated, and purchased various curling irons and other necessities of the trade. Mommy hired a carpenter and an electrician to enclose the veranda using big, slatted windows for light and much-needed ventilation. She separated the veranda's interior with a particle-board, creating a modest waiting area and a private work section. Daddy installed the plumbing, a sink, and other necessities. The painting was a cooperative family effort. Mommy prized ferns. Potted ferns of various kinds sat within a couple of burnished brass vases on small, polished tables. Ivies she let grow down from hanging baskets. She had her diploma professionally framed and mounted. "Apex Beauty Parlor" the red, white, and green calligraphed sign advertised, and at the lower left, in small lettering, it read, "Madame E. King, Beautician."

The enterprise pulled customers like a magnet. In addition to Mommy's skills, Apex had by far the best location, in the heart of the town, and great customer service. One got beautified at the time she or he chose, each date entered within Mommy's appointment book. Mommy worked with admirable assiduousness, strength, and dogged perseverance. Sometimes she would do an entire wedding party, hair, and facials—on schedule.

When the annual three-day fair, major dances, or other such occasions arrived, she would often work from midmorning into the wee hours—standing! Mommy gave out the laundry and focused on her booming parlor. She began to teach others, on their payment of course. She taught the course to her longtime friend Doris and my sister Carmen and shared profits with them. That helped her gain influence, which she leveraged well. But notice a curious development. Guess who made up the bulk of her regular customers? The very people who worked in White people's kitchens. Yes, the jobs Daddy derided. Be politically conscious or haughty as you wish, one cannot have it both ways. Do not look down on your own labor or that of others, and certainly be appreciative of those who provide your dinner. But for Mommy's enterprise and patronage of the cooks, maids and others, Pinkey might not have seen the entrance to high school. Dennis and Cecil might not have had the benefit of four years of paid tuition at semi-private Echols High School (later expanded to MacKenzie High School) nor could they have been privileged to sail on a two-week vacation to Trinidad. Carmen might not have made it to England, Dennis might never have had the opportunity prosper. Every one of us benefitted from Mommy's industry and vital social connections.

Mommy's creative imagination led to further success. She did what no other parlor had even thought of—self-promotion and business advertising through her graduates. She trained stylists in small groups of two or three per day. As they gained proficiency, they assisted with preparatory work like shampooing, first-press, and the like. For graduations, she rented the union hall and decorated it with streamers and banners, potted palms, and ferns. The local part-time printer was commissioned for invitations, programs, and tickets. Once Dennis was included for a poetry presentation. A profitable graduation dance with full bar and buffet closed the night.

Mommy exploited every legal avenue of financial benefit available. She acquired a showcase from which she sold sundry hair care items. The trademarked dressings, Black&White and Posner were expensive. That provided an avenue for financial benefit. She sent me to the pharmacy, from which I purchased Vaseline, brown and white, lanolin, oil of roses, and other fragrant extracts. Bet you already guessed that the mixer would be me. Once composed, the pomade was retailed in recycled small jars or cans. Never a worry, it was the same concoction she used in her parlor on every client. She and I did the same with the scented shampoo used in her parlor. All of these products were made in her kitchen. She taught me to clean and burnish brass vases; how to make-like-new the hair straightening and curling irons. I never minded that. With a piece of hacksaw blade and some coarse and fine sandpaper, I would make her tools shine again. She would be so pleased she'd kiss my cheek and often give me a "matinee bill." (dialectic term for the cost of a movie ticket). I was proud that she thought highly of my work.

And like us children, others certainly benefited from my mother's endeavors. If one were interested, the distribution of the earnings could be tracked and presented graphically. The earnings of those domestic workers would spread through Apex Beauty Parlor, the pharmacy, the printery, and the haberdashery. Those mother's earnings went to support of a young child's schooling hundreds of miles away in a coastal village, giving him a leg up in life and sparing him the cane or paddy fields. Their labor might have bought a daughter her school uniforms and books, improving her self-esteem and preparing her to, one day, be ready for the opportunity to become an engineer.

Mommy liked popular melodies. The last I know of was "Sukiyaki," a Japanese pop song by Kyu Sakamoto. Her favorite vocalists were Nat King Cole, Ray Charles, Louis Armstrong, and Fats Domino. She had great appreciation for Perez Prado and for brass bands in general, her local delight being Washboards Orchestra. The wail of the saxophone when they played "Cherry Pink and Apple Blossoms White" and "Bésame Mucho" was so pleasing.

Among her special movies was Imitation of Life. Unlike Daddy, Mommy did not follow the news, but she was politically in tune. She could identify the members of the English monarchy and our local political figures.

There are various things one may be obsessed with that to others would seem at a minimum, well, strange. To the degree that Daddy was committed to the BBC news at noon, Mommy was obsessed with Radio

Demerara's "Announcements of Deaths and Messages." Five deaths were unremarkable, as long as she did not have acquaintance with the departed. Should the broadcaster state that there were, say, sixteen, she would be visibly shaken. Should the broadcaster state that there was a major traffic accident with multiple fatalities her alarm was something to behold. Mommy knew all the notoriously dangerous roads or turns in the entire country and would proceed to discuss the place and what might have been the cause of the accident. It did not help that we lived in a heavy-industry town, where folks perished above normal rates. She took each death like that of a relative, wanted to know specifics, and presented unusually strong emotional responses.

I explained family life cycle earlier. The same is true of business. After some years Apex had reached its zenith, and Mommy sensed it. She began preparing for travel to the United States. She believed that a course in beauty and cosmetology and a course in weaving and coloring would revitalize her business. She began saving, seeking schools, and filing out immigration applications. It was, by all measures, a good idea and venture. I remember well the evening when she departed for the United States.

Mommy wrote often from East Orange, New Jersey. We knew she was well and that she'd found a job at a hospital, which she did together with school. She must have been so tired.

But adversity stalks enterprise as much as one person envies another's industry. Such a person benefits in no way, yet he or she expends tremendous energy, for free, just for the satisfaction of witnessing another's distress. Mommy believed that someone called United States Customs and Immigration. Confronted she opted to pay her flight back rather than face deportation. She had twenty-one days to leave or go to court. The school helped as much as possible, facilitating a crash course. It was a major financial and emotional hit for the whole family.

Mommy arrived home dejected but determined to make the best of it. We were so excited to see her, but her competitors and their canine bone couriers were beside themselves with glee. They—who ventured nothing, neither gained nor lost zip, their highest aspiration to tread water—were most forthcoming with merciless, excoriate gossip. What they didn't know, well, they just made-up. It wore on her. She continued with the beauty parlor, but the wind was against her and presaged ill for Apex's regeneration. Styles changed, customers were fewer, and discouraged she had changed noticeably. The business and our family were in the unmistakable stage of decline. If one were to seek specific cause or causes, then be welcome to a fool's errand.

With Carmen, Dennis, and Cecil gone, our family could have managed just as well as we had before. But money was not the problem. Then, we might ask, what did cause such great upheaval? I do not know.

It could not have helped that midlife pressures, the inevitable questions of life's promise and meaning, wanting to know if this is all; what is there to look forward to, would be typical internal dialogues at that stage of their lives and marriage. Coincidentally, my parents' questioning and evaluation of themselves came at a time when their children were leaving, emptying the nest as they say.

But I believe that Mommy had seen other possibilities. She had seen other ways in which women could achieve. She'd learned that she need not settle for the drudgery of the kitchen, the laundry, or the fast-fading hair parlor. These observations, conjectures if you will, are germane to understanding possible reasons for the breakdown of their marriage and business.

CHAPTER XXVI

INTERLOCK EFFECTUATED

CLAIM ON KINSHIP and reciprocal relationships were crucial in hunter-gather and agrarian societies. Among the benefits of these bonds were protection of life; protection of territory with water and food supplies; and, of course, genetic transmission. That was pretty basic. All else, for example what becomes of a widow and her children, expression of filial piety, and so on are best left to sociologists, anthropologists, philosophers, and professional debaters. All I ask is that elitist spun pejoratives about "savage man" and "man in state of nature" B be given a rest and buried by aristocrats and their ilk. (Their marriages, of course, were the means by which they protected and expanded their influence, wealth and privilege, certainly not for whimsical love.)

Some folks engage in discourses on the relevance of kinship and other human bonds in an advanced society like ours. Chatting with a friend recently about what she thought to be her personal independence, I asked the simple question, "Should you have a sudden problem with your car, how many phone calls do you expect to make before normalcy of your life is restored?" Think about that for a while; tally up how many different actions and consequences stem from that singular event. For some, the problem is very unlikely to ever occur. For others taking care of the problem and resuming "normal" life takes a single call. For so many, many of us, it's only the beginning of a cascade of misfortunes. It is vital to have a sister or know a friend who knows someone whose uncle could come over tomorrow and see what he can do. Consider for yourself what other tumbles could befall you just because your mulish car threw a tantrum and refused to roll another inch. Of course there are sheltered souls who counter that it would have been prevented had the car been properly maintained. To the proponents of that line, my retort is, give yourself time.

Human interconnectedness is well beyond kinship and reciprocal duty. I believe, that it is through respectful kinship behavior that the web of humanity is strengthened as each person's altruism flourishes. Interdependence can only increase as technology advances. Until we are prepared to give up on procreation and shoot granny aback the shed, arguments about personal independence remain specious and suspect.

Sorry, I got carried away there. I'll lighten up. Earlier, I wrote about our grandmother having followed her mother to the almshouse. And I mentioned that my siblings and I had vowed that this King generation will break the cycle of disregard for the welfare of our elderly. The reader might be assuming that we acted merely from self-interest, but I'd much rather stand accused of that than to live with conscience's incessant, pitiless stings. One must be aware of parents' needs and be attentive even before critical care is necessary; one must anticipate their needs and have a plan ready to alleviate them. This is not a function of government.

It would have been nice if our parents had stayed together. I wish it had been so. Among the advantages in terms of my siblings and I caring for them as they aged, would have been that all the help could have been directed at a single home. Also, it would have been great to visit with our kids, to watch them play, and bring joy to the entire family. We definitely lost opportunities for togetherness and the intimacy of knowing each other again at different stages of our devolvement—that is to say, personal growth, kinship bonding, and inter-generational twining. What we missed, we lost forever.

Both of my parents were to die of cancer, like too many of the residents of the industrial town.

Daddy completed his house and settled on a large piece of virgin land accessible because of the new highway connecting McKenzie to Georgetown. The house sat on top of a hill and high on stilts, allowing him his hammock for his afternoon relaxation. His self-financed retirement home consisted of two bedrooms, a spacious sitting room, a kitchenette, and a bathroom. It was bright and airy, thanks to the tall windows to the front and left side.

Our father lived there several years and enjoyed his hobby farm. He raised chickens and harvested pineapples, limes, papayas, and greens. He did not need the harvest for subsistence, since his pension and savings were more than sufficient. Pinkey lived there with him for a couple of years, until she had to leave for a job opportunity with the government, but she visited often helping with house cleaning, his laundry and such. Perhaps most important was that he had someone to talk with. He never said or otherwise indicated that he was unhappy or isolated there. He did his own cooking, washing, and whatever was necessary, but spry though he was, a bladder problem bothered him. Better-qualified doctors than the ones he'd previously seen advised us that his ailment was caused by a misdiagnosed prostatic condition, and a botched operation had exacerbated it.

Situations like my father's demonstrate how the duty of kin, beginning with children, comes into play. Adult children must not only assist aged parents physically. They must also be prescient as to their needs and help them make decisions that suit the occasions. It's important to respect the person's agency, to probe delicately, and to understand his or her reticence to fully engage with efforts to aid him or her and divulge his or her circumstances. Be cognizant of the fact that a person's thinking at that stage of life is different in terms of what needs to be carried out and how. Remember, they are you.

Immediately after Mommy's partner's funeral, she was invited to come live with me and did so without hesitation. This occurred after her diagnosis of a terminal condition. She resided with Fiona, Marvin, and me in Springlands, Berbice. She had her own room and meals prepared for her.

Following a position reassignment, we moved together to Cove and John, on the East Coast Demerara, about ninety miles away. Some months later, needing more personal attention, Mommy moved to Georgetown and lived under

Pinkey's care and the spiritual ministry of her lifelong friend, Doris.

It was about six months later that Mommy died quietly. All of her children were present at her service and interment. Daddy came too, his grief at her passing unmistakable despite his usual introspective nature. After the rites, he sat on a nearby tomb for a long time, his head bowed low, lost in deep thought. Finally, at the sealing of her resting chamber, he said sorrowfully, his voice low and betraying a trace of finality, "Well, Elaine. It's all over now." It was not until nineteen years later that he followed her.

Our family determined that, despite Daddy's protestations, it was no longer safe for him to live in the area he loved so much. One consideration was the fact that others with villainous intent were aware of his sojourn in Barbados and recently in the United States. Their kind would assume him to be wealthy and an easy mark. Just as concerning, should he take ill, there was no one in the home to aid or get him emergency medical care.

Pinkey coaxed him into leaving his beloved dwelling and abide with her in Georgetown. There he enjoyed his own room, conveniences, security, and camaraderie for several years. Not being presumptuous, but taking everything I know of my father, I believe those were most likely the best years of his life. I visited him three times since my migration to the United States. He was as spirited as ever. On my departures, usually at 4:00 a.m., he would sit up in bed to say good-bye. I would hug him; he would place his hands on my head and bless me with a good life and prosperity. He was very frail then. It was a dreadful, emotional experience each time thinking it was sure to be our last good-bye. That was the home Daddy died in. In a strange twist, it's also the same room, the same bed from which Mommy had departed our world nearly two decades earlier—both, with the support of their six children and in Pinkey's care. She remembers the day she took Daddy to the doctor. After his examination, the doctor gave Pinkey a document. It stated a diagnosis of cancer and how he proposed to treat it. According to Pinkey, it was shortly after leaving his office that, Daddy said to her, "I know what's in the paper the doctor gave to you. I know because, when I took my father to his doctor, he did the very same thing." That is to say, the doctor gave my father the diagnosis of my grandfather.

This time, both parents were well cared for until they left this world. Our filial duty was honored. We opened the door of the musty, overcrowded closet and let all the skeletons go free.

IMPERFECT
Family
Setting Free Skeleton Of Kinship Neglect

Time spent with your children is precious. Just being at home regularly and talking about whatever is sufficient for the emotional development and comfort of every member of the family. Just talk.

This family saga is about an ordinary family's cohesiveness, strength, ambition, and determination that made it possible for within one generation to climb the slippery, ramshackle ladder from deprivation to the security of American middle-class. The story accentuates what has been said by many others, that poverty is more a matter of perception and relativity; that with understanding one's situation thoroughly, one might find a way from victim to mastery through right thinking, right actions, and reciprocity. The author is not seeking to assert that everyone can bootstrap a way out of poverty. There are places and situations so bereft of opportunities, where poverty is so abject, it will be a travesty to even suggest that behaviors on their part could lift them out. With Several years of experience as a Commissioned police officer and a second career as a Child Protective Investigations Program Administrator, the author, having visited the homes of thousands of families, interviewing many, many more individuals, has come to believe what for some is already known at an intellectual level, that there are no perfect families.

The author of this family saga has a unique perspective of what helps families. Having visited thousands of homes in professional contexts he is not jaded in asserting that there are no perfect families, but there are multitudes of families who are adroit at concealing the unflattering while parading what they believe to be commendable. He accepts that today, much is beyond the capacities of families who struggle, but there are precepts that if understood and honored, may at least alleviate some of their burdens. Reaching back objectively, to his Irish Great Grandfather and Great Grandmother of African ancestry, the author is deliberate in making key assumptions that the ethics of plantocracy resonate onto our time, and that intergenerational abuse and kinship disregard exacerbate our situation. Told in the style of a participant observer, examining certain decisions made and their tragic consequences, yet the writer skillfully managed and interspersed the story with very amusing episodes and folklore.

LEYLAND A. KING, Superintendent of Police (Fmr.) Child Protective Investigations Program Administrator(Ret.) holds a Master's Degree in Mental Health Counseling and Agency Development from Troy State University. He is also a Certified Public Manager. Mr. King resides with his family in Florida, USA. Mr. King may be contacted through his blog," BlueGadfly.com.

EPILOGUE
Chapter 1

ON THE UNNECESSARY URGENCY TO LET GO

A languorous lolling; rolling, rocking along on that rusty, battered train of the puzzled, well some of them were that way, which I joined seven decades ago in third class, and later realizing that fellow passengers got on and off at will. Inscrutable each and implacable all.

-The thought, the bud, the flowering the soliloquy, the torrential tragedy.

The trip's early portion had its impatience. Presumptuously urging, pleading, boorishly insistent as I fussed, frustrated myself, overly critical of progressing at a snail's unbustled pace.

Somewhere approaching the twentieth distance-plus-time marker, my crabbiness subsided and mysteriously never visited me again. But what replaced the ornery impatience to get to what I thought would be my autonomy, was the compulsion with the chase that afflicts youth. Only youth, it seems. Like the heated dog's desire to indiscriminately rush upon all and any cars on what he thought to be his exclusive block. I just had to exhaust myself similarly. Masterfully! Panting my way, keeping my dangling, dragging leash-chain safe from trespassing others. Yes, that I easily accomplished but sometimes to my chagrin.

The train's canter bothered me none. See, it's still unclear to me which was the cost, and which was the privilege. In the blind, heated moments of the chase's reasoning, caution and sobriety are no longer monitors, and god, some cars I painfully regretted ever getting entangled with. Wrong dog, and wrong car. A squishy mess to behold.

On reflection, I admit that the train now appears to be hurtling, insatiably gobbling up miles somewhere along mile marker fifty-nine. When did it transform itself to what now seems like a reckless bullet train? I wish it'd slow so that I may appreciate bucolic, rustic farm-country rolling by. Now, all green fields and freshly plowed land flash by. It mattered to none but me, what was being missed. Well, so it seemed then. What's the rush? What's the frantic urge? I demand, I beg. Why fly past the weeping woman, forlorn with her three children standing in the cold on the shadowed station-platform?

I yearned to be able to discern the indiscernible, to have pictures, tactile momentous pleasures, and the swift vanishing memory-less past, -to mourn. But most of all, like most of us, I just wish that I had had more time. A little more youthful time.

REFLECTIONS ON THE NARRATIVES OF THIS BOOK, IMPERFECT FAMILY.

The son builds for himself and his purposes an elaborate, elevated, gilded castle at no cost to his own purse. Then he declares its own perfection. "A castle deserves a King," says he. "A king must also have a Family and a Dauphin".

Much later, to the one who shall also be crowned, the Dauphin, is struck by a self-serving provocative thought that he is not obliged to wait. He never promised anyone anything, anyway, not even to good manners or tradition, did he ever commit. He reasons and he absolves.

The Dauphin bloodily wars his way onto the throne and declares himself a hero and a King. Appellated to his name is, "the Great", and from that unscrupulous moment on, the erstwhile convicted father is again and over again put on a prejudicial trial by the throne for any and everything done, mis-done and not done.

Such is the literary history of the father-son relationship that extends its annals to this day. The son slays his father, sometimes figuratively, while he protects and forgives the doubtful reputation of his mother -literally! That is the Law of the Family. The irrepressible power of the past as understood by philosophers and Aeschylus. The father has himself the son, the heir -an extension of himself, and progenitor. The son demands the same but must free himself of the father's shadow. Guilt is washed away by the near sacred, inviolable love directed towards the flawless mother.

Chapter 2

"It is easier to build strong children, than to repair broken men."

- Frederick Douglass.

It is the time of second guessing and mistaken thinking, judging and sometimes regretting. Confusion about what's past, and imperfections- I anticipate much difficulty with this, my particular objective of presenting the appropriate measure of openness. What is just right for readers' interests and clarity. What is already in the foreground that might be improved; what has happened since the original publication of Imperfect Family. In attempting to expand upon such, would that be risking a bit too wild a turn thus making this epilogue into an elaborate elegy. I assure you that my intention is much more straight-forward and distant from that. I want only a modest chance to leave my postural inspiration. I'll use my own poetry to assert my thinking at this poignant time of my life, because they save us time.

Chapter 3

DARE TO RISK AND TO WIN. WITHOUT RISK ONE HAS ALREADY LOST.

I never thought that I would be in this, the third of my stages of life. I shall be seventy-five years old and happy. So far, I have conquered mental illness and continue to carefully manage anxiety's symptoms. Stress exacerbates anxiety. I have also successfully overcome cancer. I pronounce myself healthy and happy.

I do not care for the celebration, though if loved ones insist, I will be polite and respectful of their wishes and the occasion. I will smile fondly pretending some vague, hidden knowledge which I do not have, like hoary headed ancestors seemingly possessed and to master their own display. Thereafter, a book crowns the evening's occasion.

Chapter 4

Be glad of your own successes, for there are so many to count and maybe to come, for nature diligently plucks early all useless things.

Fictional tales would have believers consume success stories of heroic characters who left their homes on exploratory pursuits, made by a hero who knew nothing except a mythic tale and the world's four cardinal points.

Nevertheless, he gets there despite his own ignorance and trials, he overcomes, and returns to his homeland in great adulatory celebration.

Life is nothing of the kind. Hard work, determination, and hard purposeless work, produces nothing more than tremendous tragedies of disappointment.

Hard work + knowledge+ determination + opportunity (might) =success. But is that all? For if the social theory is correct, then it will prove fortuitous every time. So, it is a useful myth, mostly because it works sometimes and the beneficiary is then able to preen proudly and declare that self attributed nonsense most often prated in America - "I worked hard, paid my taxes and played by the rules." Hence success. But success, however defined by the individual, just does not always work that way for there are way too many variables, catapults and unsurvivable traps.

I position the above to concisely address the coming questions about notions on migration, attribution, character and the often-underrepresented issues of counsel, advice, support, mentoring and influence. The most commonly ignored questions when one considers that which is due exclusively to themselves or not. Let's look at the theoretical self attribution fallacy- A student gets a good grade on a test and tells herself that she studied hard or is good at the material. She gets a bad grade on another test and says the teacher doesn't like her or the test was unfair. Athletes win a game and attribute their win to hard work and practice.

To elaborate, failure has no known father.

For children preserve the fame of a man after his death.
    "To everything there is a season, and a time to every purpose...."

ECCLESIASTES: 3: 1-8-KJV.

Chapter 5

OF THE MEN QUINTESSENTIAL WHO KNEW WHAT TO SAY

"Cast your nets on the other side….."

LUKE 5: 1-11

The Police Force Makes the Man; America Takes His Measure

On his way leaving our home, Uncle Ivan stopped and spoke with me in our front yard. He asked whether I had found a job and I replied, "…no, but I'm still looking". I was 18 years old at the time. I related my experiences and that the daily efforts I had been making served nothing. He was silent while contemplating the distant hilly horizon across the Demerara River. He must've known of my efforts, but then our memorable conversation began. Briefly, quietly, he said to me, "Why don't you try the police force, the fire department, and the prison service. You might find success there. Being at home here with nothing to do is not good for you." We talked a bit more when I committed myself to do as he had suggested.

The late Ivan Thornhill, Uncle Ivan, to us was social kin, had served in the British West Indian Army, fought in Palestine and Aden where he was badly wounded. He had an amazing, contemplative type of confidence somewhat lacking in my personality, but then again, though I was already taller than him, self confidence for me, was very late in coming. A psychological trait not uncommon in abused and neglected children paying the price of their own victimization.... but the payments are on lengthy, cruel installment plans.

That night, I recall writing three applications to the said agencies and would you believe it within a month I was notified of my selection for an interview and the process started towards the result you already know. The police force.

Blessings don't easily cluster, I venture into this realm trepidatiously because evidence is overwhelmingly absent, however. I recall the assistance of a police detective (U.L) pushing my name into the newly forming Forensic Science Department. I was quite qualified for it, more so than most of the others rightfully selected. But for him to quietly advocate on my behalf was much appreciated and brought me to notice as a respected detective.

My third experience along the same lines accord with a senior officer, within our division, about changing my life's trajectory. In his case, it was more of the persistence that eventually led me into the direction he was seeing. He seemed to have a vision of my future and was determined to sway me to perceive things the way that he did. And very persuasive he seemed. But I would have none of it. I had no interest in leaving the country. I had no interest in going to the United States, and in fact, I just loved my louche, little life. One not quite dissolute, but not quite wholesome either. But (G.P) never gave up on presenting more and more then substantially more reasons for me to migrate to the United States. He never got frustrated and never gave up. Finally, we agreed that I go test the waters of a three week vacation, which I did and the rest is my history.

So, what was it about these three men, none acquainted with the other and with no knowledge of each other's actions that just kept propelling me on and upward so much? Beyond their similarities in behavioral and psychological characteristics, I really don't know.

Retrospectively, I now believe that I lacked the confidence to make upward- forward leaps. I repeat: a child pays the price of his own physical and psychological distress. His own sense of self and capabilities are rudely diminished. He settles for what is. I can think of no bold, signal advance that has been entirely of my own volition. In any competitive situation, I was always most comfortable with being third. But my benefactor was not merely saying, "I think you'll do better there". He said, "I know that you would be very successful over there". There, being the United States of America.

These kin-like men had learned the doors, held keys and opened doors at which I had balked. That's what real men do. That's what influential older men do, as benefactors of the younger.

I regard casting "your nets on the other side" and its variables, as one parable about faith, perseverance, and opportunity. Parables, like other precepts, are philosophically instructive. I believe that in the cases of Uncle Ivan and Officers (U.L and G.P) they all saw my readiness for broader possibilities "on the other side." On the other side where opportunities for success and personal growth are more abundant. To these worldly men I shall always be grateful.

Chapter 6

Transitioning from Commissioned Police Officer to Child Protection Administrator

The world is an environment. Do what is your will because it is your will, what you wish to be and to see.

Success is the easing of one's suffering, not necessarily happiness or retirement from life's toils or troubles....

Some readers wanted to know more of:

1. How did I respond to life as an administrative police officer?

2. How much did you have to change from your role as a police administrator, to that of a social services administrator.

3. What advice would you like to give to a youth considering migrating to the United States.

4. Police Forces tend to be traditional, and bounded institutions practically governed by themselves. They grudgingly change.

Police are self-protective, not easily restrained or managed. They, whether it is Guyana, Boston Massachusetts, New York City and Boroughs, or other they are, if put to scale, fundamentally flawed systems of the same kind.

It is this simple: if the agency is beset with frequent complaints and scandals, then the agency is itself scandalous. Perhaps totally disreputable and organizationally bankrupt.

I believe that I responded exceptionally well to the challenges of being a Commissioned Officer in the Guyana Police Force.

I discovered that I am deeply sympathetic and acutely sensitive to abuse of police physical power. I found that it was not the legal repercussions that nettled me, for most people do not complain, but where does the anger go and when does it end, is the rage towards the police perpetrators is the wrong generalized and attributed to every policeman and woman, while robbing the reputation of the institution. Then arrives the worst outcome of all: that being, it is useless to complain and seek redress. Brutality now truly has wide and free reign.

The second and last observation as to readers needing to know of the organization's impact on my personal development and psychology is the degree of tolerance offered to drunkenness and full blown alcoholics who remain in service no matter what. These men, whatever their weaknesses associated with their addictions have little to look forward to but their own retirement, regardless of the length or time before eligibility. The afflicted might be found in every district. Usually he is removed to a dullard's position in some remote town and there he remains untouched ever again. Consideration for the man and his family? I doubt it. Here are two instances.

Annotation of Constable Charles's Case

I was off-duty and in plain clothes when having left a friend's home about 9.00 P.M one breezy, harvest-moon night, I chose to turn right instead of left, cycling my way just to enjoy that beautiful view of the countryside. Happenstance intervened I suppose. Two curves along the road and suddenly I heard the yelling commonly associated with an altercation. The scene was thus: In a dry trench-bed I witnessed a beating.

The hapless victim I recognized as Constable Charles, age about twenty six, plumbing six feet, lean and fit. He was my barracks mate. Charles was at the receiving end of four paling staves likely ripped from some nearby fence. He was enclosed by four young men, all youths of nearby villages. The greatest danger to him, situated lower, his assailants on higher ground, was that he was cornered and clearly wearing. It appeared that they hadn't seen or heard my arrival. I shouted, they swung and crouched. Charles managed to get behind me, my bicycle positioned to protect both of us. I quickly engaged talking our way out. Talking mellows the furious beast- sometimes. I would add character and respect, help more than credited.

The dialogue revealed that the five had been imbibed with rum, when allegedly, the policeman had made a churlish comment. That was sufficient for the brawl. First punches and escalation to armed beating.

The bargain I made with the four miscreants was that I report the incident. Of course, I did. I never saw my mate again.

Annotation of Constable Babb's Case

This also involved consuming rum to excess. Babb was my friend and colleague of the same police station. This incident occurred within one year of the first.

Succinctly, the constable demanded the purchase of a second container of alcohol, his acquaintance refused, he beat the fellow, arrested him and secured him in the lockup. Later that night the victim died of injuries to his head. Constable Babb was arrested and convicted for manslaughter. His career ended in a fifteen year prison sentence.

On My Gratitude

From dark, dust arrive'
Without a plan came I,
A tenuous claim to life
My charge be to strive
I must survive!

Frail in my worthiness
A heartbeat from nonentity
Sweet breath, a genesis.
Life! Oh, Life!
Life's marvelous light!

Naked, blind, mute, penniless,
Such was I deliver'
Naught for my neediness.
Help assumed by another
A dutiful father, a caring mother.

God gave me significance.
Never alone was I ever,
From me evolved us
And I became we
Safe in our blessed family.

Transitions will always come subjectively and within unique circumstances. I believe that no two situations can ever be identical, just as no two individuals can be physically identical or in behavioral terms. I extend that analogy to explain the fact that however close individuals might be, there is no surety that they behave the same in given environments. Persons are also known to respond differently in varying situations, therefore, similarities of actions in. two or more environments are as far as we might dare go scientifically.

The fact is that my transitioning, actually began in Guyana at the point of conception of the idea, when I decided to migrate; thoughts changed, planning began. Thoughts changed, in the sense that I had already proved myself competitively through the University of Guyana and the Police Force simultaneously. Now I had both knowledge and practice for the world out there.

To be honest, it was stressful. I needed to upgrade my qualifications and meanwhile support my family all in the midst of moving from New York City, to Florida for a better environment. Since this has been included previously, I shall continue only as to what has been asked: that is to say, the experience of adapting from police to social services matters.

Close relationships are there between police departments in the United States and the Social Services Agencies. This is because they both serve the public good through the laws of the various states and some funding by way of the Federal Government. Additionally, laws pertaining to violence against women and children are enforceable by the said departments. However, whereas police powers tend to focus on criminal laws with possibilities of arrest and detention, the social services laws focus on ensuring voluntary compliance with the agency to prevent further breaches of the laws. Both departments could use various processes to bring the Court's powers to bear.

The investigative means are broadly similar, and after seventeen years in that career with the State of Florida, illness's persistent calls said it was time for me to leave.

The End

www.ingramcontent.com/pod-product-compliance
Lightning Source LLC
LaVergne TN
LVHW010155070526
838199LV00062B/4369